BRIGHT
YELLOW

BRIGHT YELLOW

A BOOK ABOUT
INDEPENDENCE AND SPIRIT

BARBARA SVEDAHL

MILL CITY PRESS, MINNEAPOLIS

Mill City Press, Inc.
322 First Avenue N, 5th floor
Minneapolis, MN 55401
612.455.2293
www.millcitypublishing.com

ISBN-13: 978-1-63413-918-2
LCCN: 2016900245

Cover Design by B. Cook
Typeset by MK Ross

Cover photo: Barb and Carol at their
2005 class reunion

Printed in the United States of America

Dedicated to Mother

PROLOGUE

They were lined up on the pew, all eight of them— the dogs Mother had trained in her obedience school to become therapy dogs. They were sitting so politely, wearing their black bandanas. Everyone was so very moved, and not one of the dogs made a sound. When the service ended, all eight dogs followed in a line to the front of the altar and sat next to her urn among the many bouquets of flowers. Pictures were taken. I knew I would treasure them, and I knew Mother would have been most proud of this tribute. The dogs had meant the world to her.

During the service, Carol and I stood up and shared stories about our growing up with Mother— Uncle Russ and his trained seal Snorky, my cat Mr. Tom, her elaborate dinner parties. Pam Serdar, the pastor at Centenary United Methodist Church in Mankato, said it was the most touching funeral she had ever given.

My sister, my dear friend Carol, and I handled the funeral arrangements. Carol greeted everyone as they entered the church and handed out the programs. Following the service was a luncheon catered from a local restaurant. I was happy to see my cousin Pam and her husband. They had come to town from their retirement home in Florida, and they had both thought the world of Mother. And to think we were all women who made it happen.

Her ashes were spread in my garden among the flowers she had always admired and where my family's pets are buried. I wasn't sure if this was the right resting place for Mother, but I thought she would be happy with that decision. Once again, I listened to her: "Do what you think is right." These encouraging words of hers have helped me through much of my life.

CHAPTER 1

I was five on that day in 1948 when Mother pulled out the map of Minnesota, closed her eyes, and placed a finger randomly. It ended up near the bottom. That's where Mother, my sister, and I would be going—without Dad. We were going to do everything without Dad, now that my parents were divorced. I could tell Mother was very unhappy, but I was too young to understand why. All I knew was that it was time to leave Iowa and begin our new life. I said goodbye to my cousins Linda and Joann and began to feel an emptiness.

We moved to an apartment above the Coast to Coast Hardware in Mankato, Minnesota. This is where I would play and ride my little tricycle up and down the dark hallway. Our apartment was on the third floor facing Main Street and was much different from our old house with its large yard and trees. Maybe I thought this move was temporary, but it wasn't. My world was changing.

John and Frieda Turner lived in the apartment next to ours. John was an artist and becoming well known for his paintings. During the time we were neighbors, he gave Mother painting lessons. I have a likeness of me she painted on a yellow dinner plate. We couldn't have asked for better neighbors while starting out in our new surroundings.

I had brought with me my white stuffed cat that I got for Christmas the year before. He had a long limp tail and gold button eyes. Whiskers was there for me; he would be my friend now. Over time, half his fur wore away, and he no longer looked like an Angora, but no matter how straggly, he was well loved.

The 1950s was a difficult time for a single woman raising daughters. With $60 a month child support, we did the best we could to make a new life. We didn't have a car; we relied on the city bus. This was all so very different from our life in Iowa. However, Mother had a plan for our future and the determination to make it work.

Mother had learned her domestic skills at the age of sixteen while living with the family of Reverend Wiener in southern Minnesota as their cook, sitter, and seamstress. She relied on this experience to carry her through her life. Our clothes were made from the many patterns she collected, but she also made changes to them to fit her individual style. I never felt inferior wearing the clothes she made for me, and I had many choices. An aunt in Iowa once said, "Your mother looks like she just stepped out of a bandbox." At the time I didn't know what that meant, but I knew it had something to do with how pretty she was. Mother often relaxed as I combed her long dark hair and played with it before she brushed it away from her face and twisted it back in a loose knot. The contrast of her hair with her features really added to her beauty.

Her father preached in a small Episcopal church in a nearby town. My sister and I sat in the creaky balcony and listened to Grandfather's sermons. Mother sang in the choir. She had a beautiful voice, but I couldn't help watching her throat as she sang; it jiggled, and I wished she'd lower her voice and not draw attention to herself. She wore dangling earrings, which I didn't think were right for church. This awareness would be the beginning of the interesting life I would have with my mother. Grandfather's health was declining, and when I was nine, he was diagnosed with malignant brain cancer. Unfortunately I don't have many other memories of him other than visits to the nursing home, and even then I was often only allowed to stand outside on the lawn and look up at his window, hoping he could see me.

I entered first grade without a hitch. I was eager to make new friends and begin a school year in our new town. Mother began looking for a job. She started out with a short stint as a radio dispatcher for a cab company.

Summers I rode the Greyhound bus to Storm Lake, Iowa to visit my grandmother, Matilda Flohr Hussey, my father's mother. Also to see my two cousins. Along the way I tried to raise myself up on the scratchy, worn-out seat so I could see out the small window. I was mesmerized by the rows and rows of cornstalks. They made me think of skirts flowing back and forth over miles of flat country roads that seemed to go on forever.

Grandma's house had an expansion upstairs where I slept and read books. The room was very warm with only a faint breeze flowing between the two small windows. In the living room Grandmother's porcelain dolls sat on her piano wearing hand-crocheted dresses that hung over its edge. I didn't touch them; somehow I knew I shouldn't, and I never asked.

Grandma loved making fried chicken and used lots of oil in a large pan, unlike my Mother's healthy baked version. Included with the meal were slices of ripened tomatoes covered with sugar. When Grandma ate, the juice of the tomatoes trickled from the corners of her mouth.

Each time I came to Grandma's, cousins Linda and Joann came to see me. We were only a couple of years apart, and we always had fun together. One day we made up a little tune, changing the words from "Take Me Out to the Ballgame" to "Take Me Out to the Dairy Queen." Grandma finally gave in to us after hearing the tune over and over, and she would treat us to ice cream.

Possibly the best time we had in Iowa was fishing in Lake Okoboji in Grandma's small metal boat. She wore a floppy fishing hat like the kind men wore; it covered half her face, and as hard as she tried to protect herself from the sun, her skin was always covered with freckles. She would reach into her worn tin minnow bucket and grab the minnow. I hated seeing her pierce the little creature on the sharp hook as it squirmed to be free. We always returned to her house with an assortment of tiny fish that seemed like prizes to her.

My father was a very handsome man with wavy, sandy hair, and he always dressed well. But the times we were together were becoming fewer, and my visits to Iowa eventually ended. He was seldom mentioned within my family, including by Grandma. I know Mother tried to make up for the decreasing time spent with our father, but honestly I was beginning to like our new life, and I knew Mother was trying hard to make it work.

I wouldn't consider myself as having been plain—I'll just say I was timid. When I was eight, I had my first picture taken by a photographer and chose to wear my Hopalong Cassidy vest and boots. In those days people didn't think something must be wrong if a girl was dressed as a cowboy. I also collected Storybook Dolls, a version of the Barbie doll. These were a series of dolls that came in a clear box shaped like a book and wore various outfits. They were lined up in a row in my bedroom. I didn't take them out of their boxes; I thought they were too pretty to play with.

Mother 1955

CHAPTER 2

After the cab company, Mother answered an ad for the position of home economist at Northern States Power. During her interview she was asked, "Can you conduct a cooking school?" "Can you host a radio program?" She later told me she answered "yes" to each question, regardless of whether she could or not, because she was focusing on her daughters. There wasn't anything she wasn't able to do. She was hired.

I met Carol Church (later Schaible) when we were both six, and it was through our parents. Mother enjoyed the fascinating, outgoing personality of Carol's mother, who was Greek. The women admired each other's style of home furnishings and often traded: a lamp for a lamp and a picture for a picture. Carol's dad was an architect who had designed the Mankato High School building. He was a small man who spent hours listening to classical music.

We were invited to their house for dinner; both women loved entertaining guests. At our first visit, Carol and I ate our dinner on little trays with legs that were set up in the screened porch. I was feeling very awkward with this stranger. Carol took one pea at a time from her plate and dropped it into my glass of milk. She watched me while she did this, waiting for me to say something. She was daring me to get upset, but I didn't say a word. I had already caught on to her little annoyances. Even though we came from very different backgrounds, we became pretty much inseparable as we spent more time together. We played dress-up in our beautiful gowns (or so we thought) that we put together with whatever we could scrounge up, and we argued over who would be Debbie Reynolds. Carol was a bit spoiled, being an only child, but she would be the first to admit it.

One weekend we visited her grandparents in Wisconsin. They owned a movie theater. One of the movies we watched was *Three Coins in the Fountain*. I thought we were pretty special, since we didn't have to pay admission. While her grandparents played cards in their kitchen late into the night, Carol and I stayed awake talking and giggling. When the circus came to town, we watched the show from wooden bleachers. I remember feeling sorry for all the animals, but I kept my feelings to myself. I didn't like seeing animals made to perform. Even at that young age, I wondered if they were happy, and I never went to a circus again. I've never gotten over those feelings.

Mother was enjoying her job at the power company and had already advanced to home service director. She was also given a radio program on the local station, KYSM. It was primarily a woman's show, and she was popular from the start. Women loved listening to Mother as she shared ideas for the modern homemaker such as recipes for healthy eating and laundry tips. A pet peeve of hers was soap buildup, and she offered ways to achieve a cleaner final rinse. She had a way of making everything sound like a very important life event, always using the glass-half-full reasoning.

When Carol and I were a little older, Mother had us as guests on the Thanksgiving show. She asked me, "Barbara, what are you most thankful for?" Silence. I could only stare at the large microphone in the small enclosed room. I hated to be called Barbara! She was using her professional voice to call me Barbara. I was, and still am, Barb. Mother kept looking at me and waiting. Finally Carol said, "I guess . . . nothing." It wasn't a surprise that we weren't asked to come back. I give credit to Carol's quick thinking for getting us out of ever being on Mother's show again.

There were many issues for women in the fifties. Women didn't talk about their private lives, and they paid a price for that. But their truths would have made a real talk show. I can only imagine what Mother would have said to those women if they talked about real issues. Divorces was almost unheard of and were widely frowned on. The "pill" wasn't legal until 1960, and some women who used birth control devices hid them because of their religion. The job market and lack of skills prevented a woman from getting a decent job.

A woman could be having a dreary life at home, secretly hoping to be rescued, while her husband was gone all day at work. During those years, I saw the difference between my mother and other mothers, but I never thought my life was any different from anyone else's, even without a dad.

In the building on Main Street where Mother worked was an auditorium, and there she decorated a small stage with appliances and tables and set up for demonstrations for her many events. The Hawaiian luau had everything but the grass skirts. One demonstration was given to a roomful of nuns. She commented how interested they were in what she had to say as they listened to her advice on how to do their laundry. Mother loved her job. She would share her ideas with anyone interested, and there were articles about her in the local newspaper along with large photos. Her recipes were tested and published as Reddy Kilowatt holiday recipes, mostly desserts and candies, all delicious.

Her favorite cologne was Avon's To a Wild Rose. It came in a pretty milk glass bottle with a pink stopper and was available for all to use in the women's restroom at Northern States Power. I also enjoyed splashing on a little. Another extra touch of hers.

In the fifties a newcomer, John Gallos, was just starting his career, as Clancy the Cop. Mother often shared radio time with John, this was his first time entertaining. The two personalities worked very well together. John later became successful and moved to television in the Twin Cities, where he broadcast his show over a forty-year career.

Northern States Power retailed home appliances, and a representative from General Electric came to speak to employees regarding some new products. Ronald Reagan was the representative! Disappointed in his decline in movie popularity, he had become the host of General Electric Theater in 1954, and was a big success. General Electric sent him on personal appearances, and Mankato was one of the stops.

Mother and Mr. Reagan had lunch at a local restaurant down the street from the power company, the Candy Kitchen. Ester and Eros Zotalis, the owners, were gracious and down-to-earth people. They were Greek. Ester was a petite woman who wore pretty dresses; her black hair was pulled back in a loose bun and a white apron was tied around her tiny waist. Glass candy containers filled with tempting treats lined the counter. Years later when Mr. Reagan became our president, Mother recalled, "What a gentleman he was, and how I enjoyed his company." I wonder if he bought jelly beans at the Candy Kitchen. Mother was comfortable with anyone—she was the epitome of charm and dignity.

CHAPTER 3

Carol and I attended confirmation classes in 1953 at the old stone Belgrade Avenue Methodist Church in North Mankato. We memorized and recited the books from the Old and New Testaments in the musty church basement. I thought the classes would never end. It was too nice outside to be stuck indoors, but we made it through to the end and were confirmed in the spring. I was given my own Bible and gold cross necklace with tiny rhinestones. During my life I have been a Lutheran and a Catholic. Being Catholic was like being on another planet. Now I've returned to my Methodist roots, and I'm very happy to be back.

That summer, after confirmation, Mother sent me to Camp Patterson on Lake Washington. The second day she came to take me home because I was homesick. I thought she would say something or ask a lot of questions, but she didn't say a word. That was just as bad.

The next summer was a week at a Methodist church camp. It helped that Carol was going with me. We roomed together on the third floor of a large building, and another classmate-friend, Linda Benson, was there. This time I stayed the full five days. I was beginning to build up my courage to be away from home.

The third summer, back to Camp Patterson. The rain poured through the windows even though the shutters were held up with boards. Our beds were lined up along the sides of the room and got wet. Before going to camp, I had decorated a wooden fruit crate to use for storage next to my bed. I tacked on fabric for the curtain that covered the opening, and that's where I kept everything I might need while at camp. That crate was something I was very proud of, my first creative project.

Carol has those Greek dark eyes and dark hair, and a bubbly, fun-loving personality. I've never met anyone as enthusiastic as Carol. I'm the reserved blonde—green eyes, sensitive, and very independent. We both love animals. To each other we say, they're better than most people. Connie Bills Erickson made it our threesome. Connie was the "mature" one; when she'd had enough, she would say to Carol and me with her hands on her hips, "All right for you guys." We all had a big laugh when she got after us. This would have been after we put cat food in her sloppy joe, or set an alarm clock in her purse to go off while watching a movie in the theater. She caught on to the cat food in time from the mischievous looks Carol and I exchanged. Years later, Connie's family moved to Moorhead, Minnesota. That didn't stop us from getting together, although her mother, I'm sure, was hoping it would. She never knew what the three of us would get into. Once when visiting Connie, we dyed our hair orange and the towels also got dyed orange. But her mother was a good sport and let Connie drive her 1940s car, "Ol' Bessie," around town. Connie, the mature one, was trusted, but there were big doubts about Carol and me.

Often I was alone while Mother was working, and becoming independent was second nature. My sister and I are five years apart, and she had other interests besides watching a younger sister. However, there was that one winter day (how can I forget?). It was very cold and we were walking along a sidewalk with her friends. They dared me to put my tongue on a metal fence post. So I did, and it stuck there. It was the worst, helpless feeling as I slowly pulled my tongue loose, leaving some skin attached to the metal. I can still feel it!

In third grade we moved to a townhouse—in an interesting brick row of older homes. It had a rather dark interior that brought out the imagination in me. The long stairway down to the living room was perfect for my theatrical entrances as an actress greeting her fans or just a simple child picking flowers from the ceiling and tossing them in the air. I was in a world of my own. A few blocks away was the childhood home of Maud Hart Lovelace, the author of the Betsy-Tacy book series. One of her thirteen books was named after the "Big Hill" around the corner from where we lived. Even now, each year at the end of June a Betsy-Tacy festival is held with tours of the homes in the books.

I fell in love with cats when Mother brought home a stray. While walking home from work one day, she was followed by a homeless grey cat. That cat would become our first family pet (mine, actually). Cleaned up, Mr. Tom turned out to be a gorgeous longhair cat. My goldfish, Julie and Louie, didn't count, or my pet parakeet that sat on the top of the drapery rod in the living room and pecked the aqua paint off the wall—didn't compare to Mr. Tom. This was when I began realizing there are many different kinds of love. Carol thought I was very lucky having a mother who let me have pets, something she wasn't allowed, but we knew someday that would all change, and it did when she was older.

Mr. Tom could sit straight up in my lap without tipping over. Once Carol and I saw him standing on the toilet seat with four little paws, balancing himself and doing his business. Where did he learn that? we wondered. Mr. Tom may not have been the best mouser, but I didn't care. Sometimes we saw mice in our house, and a mousetrap was set up in back of the stove. Mother said, "Looks like a mouse was trapped, and somehow it got loose." Those tiny brown eyes looking up at me, pleading for help—I let the mouse go. I set the furry critter free in the back yard. Later, I confessed to the release, and that didn't come as any surprise.

We had Mr. Tom a couple of years, right up to the day we returned from a weekend away. Mother and I were attacked by hungry fleas. The large hemp rug in our living room was home to dozens of them, jumping on our legs and biting. After treating the rug with flea killer and cleaning Mr. Tom, Mother made the decision to find my cat a new home. I hated to part with my beloved Mr. Tom. I didn't have to look far, because my third-grade teacher, Mrs. Greely, a soft-spoken, kind woman, was happy to have him and would give him a good home. Months later, Mrs. Greely told me that Mr. Tom had run away, and I could imagine only the worst.

Mother didn't waste any time finding our next pet. She had heard of a Boston bull pup that needed a home and rushed to his rescue. We named him Snip. His little snorts were different from the soft purring of a cat, supposedly caused by the shape of the soft palate which resulted in difficulty breathing, common for the bulldog breed. But I missed my cat.

I was thirteen when my sister married, and a year later my nephew Mike was born. Often I babysat, and sometimes Carol and I watched him together. He was three when he sat at my small dressing table with the three-way mirror, removing tops of jars and covers of lipsticks, sticking his little hands in everything. Carol and I applied lipstick as Mike giggled and squirmed. Then we took his picture. He was such a happy little guy, and can I still hear him yelling "Grandma" as he ran toward Mother. One time while watching Mike, I noticed something strange about his eyes. I had to get up close to see what it was and noticed tiny insects slowly moving about on his eyelids. He kept rubbing his eyes, and I couldn't imagine what was happening. Most likely they had come from his sandbox. But my main thought was how disgusting it looked.

As I was beginning junior high in 1956, Mother moved us to a house on Range Street in North Mankato—and closer to my dear friend Carol. This made me very happy. Saturdays I got on my blue-and-white Schwinn bike and rode across town to Carol's house. The basket on the front was filled with movie magazines. Fun, but I shudder now as I think of that little blonde girl pedaling across town alone.

Behind our house there was (and still is) a large park and ice skating rink, and I spent many hours there. At night its lights shone, and I warmed up in the warming house. Skating was something I always loved doing. Mother loved telling the story about me in Iowa at the age of four, skating for the first time. She laughed as she described my tiny feet flying across the rink without falling down. I knew she was proud of me, and I enjoyed listening to her tell that story.

I secretly hoped the boy living down the street would be at the rink. He often came to skate, and it always made my day. He was a classmate, very friendly and polite, and needless to say, I thought he was good looking. Many years later during a television special, I saw him introduce and joke with Bob Hope on a ship carrying our troops overseas. Mr. Parker hadn't changed much since our days on the rink—older, of course, but he still had the same drawl in his voice and the same smile. I had known he was in the military, but it still was a surprise seeing him on television, and the faint image crossed my mind of us in junior high and the skating rink.

Another memory like this was the walk down the street with the brother of a friend when I was fifteen. He was a few years older. I thought of this as the perfect thing to do on a date. Heavy flakes of snow were barely falling that evening, illuminated by the street light in the park, the park where I skated. So peaceful and quiet, except for the little swishing sound our feet made in the fresh snow. That memory crosses my mind from time to time when I need a little peaceful imagery, taking me back so many years.

Our house in North Mankato was within walking distance from school, and when school ended for the day, Rita and I walked together to my house. Rita's mother also worked and wasn't home at that time either, it became a routine, Rita and I playing at my house. Her imagination and funny stories brought out the best in me. I was a timid girl in those days, and I feel very fortunate that I had Rita for a friend. The North Mankato classmates have retained much of the closeness we had many years ago. It's evident at our class reunions—we stick together.

My mother's brother, Russ Zieske lived in St. Cloud, Minnesota was in show business for fifty years entertaining all ages as a magician. His wife Ruth was his performing assistant, and they had no problem drawing in their audiences. A favorite location was schools, especially for the younger ages, who were always happy to see his magic. One year they brought their show to my school. I was so surprised when Uncle Russ mentioned that I, his niece, was in the audience. That was a proud moment for me! Snorky was his trained seal in the magic act. Snorky could balance balls on his head, play a horn, and climb stairs. Russ would say, "Snorky would do anything if he was tossed a fish." My uncle's theatrical name was Russ Charles. He was honored by being named a member of the Northland Magic Hall of Fame.

CHAPTER 4

When Mother had dinner guests, they sat at the dining room table, and tiny glass Fostoria ashtrays were conveniently placed for people who smoked. The only problem was, I always wanted to clear the table before her guests were through eating. The cousins, my sister, and I sat at the kitchen table, and Snip, the dog, had a prime spot next to us. (That is, until he started letting off a foul smell. Mother gave him a charcoal tablet to fix his problem). Nothing she made was from a box mix, only put together from scratch. She also canned tomatoes, ketchup, peaches, and plums. Best of all was her Plum Sunshine Jam. I have tried making it, but hers was so much better. Mother didn't use margarine; she questioned what the ingredients were. She wondered why there was some kind of substance in the center, a red dot, and people were instructed to mix it into the margarine. We never knew what the purpose of that was.

I always thought it was a treat when she brought leftovers home from her cooking school demonstrations. If Carol was at our house for dinner, she would lift the lids from the pans on the stove and always rave about how good it all tasted. Carol and I would wash the plastic covers that covered the food containers and let them dry on the kitchen counter, looking like shower caps all in a row. Back then I knew there should be a better way for storage. Carol was the only person to get by with calling my mother, Millie. Everyone else used her real name, Mildred.

Saturday was my cleaning day, and I didn't leave the house until my work was finished. It was just a known fact, and I didn't need to be told. Actually, I enjoyed doing the work. My first paid job, and I thought I had really grown up, was helping a neighbor clean her house while she gave piano lessons in her home. I tried to be as careful as possible, but one day as I backed up on my hands and knees washing her kitchen floor, I knocked the cat dish straight down the basement steps. It shattered into tiny pieces. I panicked and slowly picked them up and secretly disposed of the evidence, never saying anything—until now. I was young, and it never occurred to me that I should explain what happened to their cat dish.

I worked a summer at the food counter in the local Greyhound bus depot when I was fifteen. It had me memorizing all the towns in Minnesota and beyond. I was embarrassed to make sandwiches with one slice of meat for people I knew were in need of more. Sometimes I would add an extra slice, knowing I shouldn't. My supervisor was a woman who treated me like her daughter; she wasn't married and spent most of her time at the depot. When I started working there, the building had just opened and everything was new. We actually learned how to operate everything together. The bus drivers sat for hours at the counter killing time and drinking coffee between their runs. They liked talking to me. Some told me about their families. I listened to all their stories. I suppose it got boring for them, being away from home for long periods and driving the same routes day after day.

The next summer I carhopped at the Oasis Drive-In. I enjoyed working outside, but I do remember how hooking those metal trays onto people's car windows could be very tricky while balancing heavy mugs of root beer. Carol and I worked together, and when it rained, we wore large yellow vinyl raincoats. We could visit a bit with our friends when they were our customers, a little perk while working. One evening, a friend picked me up after work in her mother's car and we headed down Main Street. We were sixteen at the time. Her eyes weren't on the road—she was looking around to see if she could spot her latest big crush. She also lacked driving experience, and so she ran into a car at the stop sign. She hit it hard. Her head hit the dashboard and a tooth flew out of her mouth. I wasn't hurt, but I knew she would be in trouble when facing her mother that night.

"Actions speak louder than words" was my mother's philosophy of discipline. There was the little nudge on the shoulder and maybe a subtle frown that reminded me I'd done something I shouldn't have. Words weren't needed to let me know I had crossed the line. Today the youths require everything spelled out for them, and then some. I believe that being raised by a single parent works well for correcting behavior; only one parent sets the rules, and so the child can't put one parent against the other.

In ninth grade, I watched Mother's health slowly decline. She tired easily. She would come home from work and cover herself with the afghan and fall asleep on the sofa. Each day her nap would last longer. I didn't want to wake her and tried to be as quiet as possible. The doctor said she was having a relapse of rheumatic fever she'd had as a child, and it was uncertain she would pull through. This seemed to last forever, but it actually went on for just one year until she completely recovered, much to her doctor's surprise. She later thanked me for letting her rest and taking care of the house. We always seemed to get by somehow. Many nights I fell asleep listening to the popular radio program, Hobb's House. A Twin Cities station offering the music style I enjoyed.

I was enrolled in Edna Pringle's dance school. Admission to her school was a great opportunity, and she required many hours of practice. I became confident in ballet. In junior high, the students gave mini-performances on stage to act out for us their seeming talent. I chose a modern dance. According to one classmate, Jeanie Anderson, I was a huge success. After that I performed at various locations in several modern dance routines, along with my ballet dancing.

My passion was ballet, and Mother's friend, Jerri Bell, took the time to make my costumes, even though she had to watch her five children. I was given money to purchase cosmetics for my stage appearances at the drugstore down the street and bought Max Factor pancake makeup and eye shadow. The salesclerk gave me a questioning look, most likely thinking I was too young for makeup. I thought to myself, let him think what he wants. That wasn't what I was buying them for. Finally, I was a solo dancer. Dressed in my layers of stiff blue netting and sequins, carrying a light blue parasol, I was enjoying my routine until, for some reason, I froze halfway through. My ankles were so weak, and I heard the audience gasp, "She can't get up on her toes!" It seemed like the routine was going on forever, and I just wanted it to end. My ballet dancing career was over.

CHAPTER 5

It was Christmas 1959, and we were opening our presents. I wanted nothing to do with the gift that was inside one of them. But I wanted to be careful how I worded it. Fur, the idea an animal was killed for their fur, really upset me. Mother had hired someone to make her grey fur coat into a vest for me and thought I would enjoy wearing it, but I never did. She was hurt, but she also respected my feelings, and through the years she even became a voice for animal rights herself. The 1960s was about to open up to a new awareness. People became voices for many issues and causes that were long overdue.

Often Carol and I got together with our friends at the Wagon Wheel Restaurant on Main Street, in a not-so-nice part of town. Jukebox, burgers, cozy booths, and the hope of seeing our latest crush. Some parents thought we were headed for destruction just by being there. And sure enough, one day Carol's dad barreled in through the front door. He didn't say a word as he dragged Carol out. At home she tried to reason with her dad, saying, "Barb can be there. Her mom doesn't care."

But Mother did care, and I stopped going too. I look back on it now and clearly see that going to the Wagon Wheel wasn't such a good idea. It was a hangout for kids who were older and Carol remembers beer being served.

Our parents needn't have worried. We were the least likely of anyone to get into trouble. Fifty years later, the Wagon Wheel is still standing, and thinking of it brings back many memories of those teenage years: the hours sitting in a booth talking with friends and making new friends over a Coke and rock 'n' roll songs playing on the jukebox. Now hats and mugs are sold as souvenirs, and the dark booths have been replaced. It's now an inviting cafe reflecting a symbol of time.

In high school, I was a member of the swim team. One day while practicing in the pool, I was overcome by another student; I'll call her Maggie.. She held me under the water as long as she possibly could while I struggled to get free of someone twice my size and then some. Our teacher finally noticed the struggle; I thought she never would. She extended a long pole out for me to grab onto while she pulled me out of the water. The cause? We both liked the same boy. He was two years older and most likely didn't know I existed. But I came close to losing my life that day over a boy who'd had a few run-ins with the law. At the time I didn't even seem to care about that.

My high school counselor advised me to focus on becoming a secretary and told me I should take lots of typing and shorthand classes to further my education. I must have fit into his stereotype mold, like so many other females he was advising. So I took his advice and enrolled for summer classes at the local business college and I could get ahead in my exciting career. Carol did the same. We sat at our typewriters pounding away on the same numbers and letters over and over to build up our speed on the second floor of the small business school downtown Mankato. Soon enough we both realized this wasn't something we wanted to do the rest of our lives.

We both registered for fall classes at Mankato State Teachers College (now Minnesota State University, Mankato). In college we made new friends. They came from towns around the area and lived in the dorms. We still didn't own a car; Mother occasionally had use of a company car but only while she was working, and college was three miles from home. I scheduled my classes close together during days I walked or rode the city bus. I didn't mind the routine and never questioned or complained. This was the chapter in my life when I focused on who I was and what was important to me. As I walked home alone, I realized that at times I felt more alone with certain people than when I was all by myself.

One evening I invited a dozen friends from college to our house. We sat on the living room floor joking around, playing cards, talking, and listening to music. Later in the evening, the police showed up at the front door because a neighbor had called to complain about a noisy party. When the officer walked in, I am sure he wasn't expecting what he saw—just kids sitting around talking. There wasn't anything to report about, and he told us to keep on doing what we were doing as he walked out the door, smiling. I knew by then to not be caught getting involved with a group that would get me in trouble.

Around this time I tried smoking my first cigarette—my first, and last. The brand back then was Kent, and it made me nauseated and dizzy. Just as bad was sitting in a room with friends who smoked. The smell clung to the air and to me. Smoking was a common thing in those days and through the sixties.

There was a group of four fellows from a rural southern Minnesota town who Carol and I got along well with and I felt they honestly enjoyed our company. They lived in a campus apartment, and Carol and I lived at home. One fellow had a new Ford convertible and gave us rides exploring the country roads where he had grown up. This was a new experience for Carol and me; we thought we were "city girls" because we lived in town. One of the four, Gene, asked me if I'd like to go for a ride in an airplane. He had his pilot's license. "Yes, I would!" I said. We went flying in the evening, and it was beautiful. Mankato is sixty miles south of the Twin Cities and the glowing lights from the city extended into the night sky and took my breath away. However, I began to question if I was doing the right thing and if he knew how to land this plane. Fortunately, he did.

For taking me up in the air with him, I surprised Gene by making a chocolate cake with rich homemade chocolate frosting, using a recipe I still use today. As I took the cake to his apartment, I didn't know what he would think of me doing this. But I got a big thank you from the guys. Who wouldn't like chocolate cake! I did wonder why a farm boy would be able to fly a plane, much less have one. I was eighteen, and very impressed. Little did I know what paths our lives would take, and that we would run into each other thirty years later in Minneapolis.

Barb at the Sibley Park Zoo, Mankato, Minnesota

Barb and sister fishing at Lake Okoboji, Iowa

CHAPTER 6

After my sophomore year in college, I thought it was time to move from home and begin working full time. Aunt Kay, Mother's sister, invited me to live with her and her husband Irv in West Des Moines, Iowa. Instead I moved into an apartment on Grand Avenue in that same part of town with my cousin Pam. Our apartment was extraordinarily nice, newly redecorated and furnished in the popular French provincial style. It had cobalt blue walls and a solarium facing the street and the stately homes. Even though we couldn't afford it, we were living in the lap of luxury. Mother suggested Pam and I sell Avon products on the weekends to add to our income. We tried doing that, but we'd end up at the same door the other one had recently knocked on, and the owner would say, "Someone else was just here." We hadn't figured out our strategy very well and gave up that idea. I don't think there was any money to be made by me selling Avon, although I did enjoy all my miniature samples I ended up paying for.

Kay and Irv were friends with the Leachman family, whose daughter, Sue, was the same age as I and we became friends. She was attending Drake University and I began classes. At the end of our semester, Sue moved to New York City to live with her Aunt Cloris, an aspiring actress, and I quit college.

The freeway sign along Interstate 35 outside of Des Moines read "Minneapolis, 250 miles north." Driving along the highway and often seeing that sign, I would have the strong sense that I would someday be living there. That feeling grew stronger each time I saw the sign, and eventually the decision was made. The day came and I packed my small Toyota with my belongings and my little white terrier, Katie, that I had adopted in Iowa, and headed to Minneapolis. Something inside me was nudging me along. I rented a small studio on Park Avenue in a lower-rent area of South Minneapolis and started job hunting.

Around that time, Mother remarried. Kay and Irv were witnesses; the small ceremony included only the family. The day before the wedding, Mother was handed papers to sign. He wouldn't marry Mother unless she signed a prenuptial agreement, which was a surprise to everyone there. Mother wasn't given any legal advice, and Kay wanted her to back out. However, Mother went ahead and signed, and the ceremony took place. The reception at a fine restaurant had an awkward, disappointed atmosphere we were all feeling. From the start, I felt a distrust for her husband, and I would prove to be right.

They began their married life along the Minnesota

River in Mankato. Prior to the spring flood of 1965, deep heavy snow had fallen, and cold weather delayed ice from melting in an orderly fashion. Up and down the Mississippi River and its tributaries like the Minnesota, people were tossing sandbags; students sixteen and over were let out of school to help. Stillwater, Minnesota sent fifty convicted volunteers from the state prison to join the battle against the flooding.

Mother's house was along the river near Sibley Park and its zoo. Animals were kept in cages, and many people in town were becoming concerned for the safety of the animals. St. Paul's Como Park offered to bring trucks to Mankato and take the animals to a safe environment. Unfortunately, that offer wasn't accepted, and the animals perished in their cages.

Mother recalled the loud knock on her front door and the warning that evacuation was underway and to collect clothing and her dog, Sam. When it was safe to return home, she discovered animal prints in the mud behind the house from larger animals that had managed to escape the zoo. Needless to say, the park lost the respect it once had and was unable to exhibit animals for many years.

Water had completely filled the basement of their house, and the old player piano had landed upside down. On the first floor, the water had risen to four feet. Mother spent months cleaning between the floorboards and door frames with a toothbrush to dislodge the residue of dry sand. After all the remodeling was finally finished, she referred to her home as her "gold-plated shithouse."

A few years later they moved to a house high on a hill overlooking the river. That house always had a welcoming feeling, with the aroma of coffee percolating—strong and black, the way she liked it. Besides Sam, her poodle, Mother had four French bulldogs, and one would always be balancing on someone's lap. Beautiful, carefully selected antiques filled the house, and a large rose garden took over the back yard. Fragrance filled the air from the cut flowers she brought inside and arranged in tall glass vases.

No longer working at Northern States Power, Mother went into the antique business, opening her shop in an old hotel building in downtown Mankato. She also worked the out-of-town antique shows and traveled with a partner who owned a hair salon. Carol once said, "Only your mother would travel with her own personal hairdresser."

Aunt Kay moved to London, England, for two years, and that was Mother's golden opportunity. While visiting there, Mother's long-time love for the black London cabs grew to the point where she sought out the company and bought her own cab. She figured out the shipping and the point of entry as Detroit. The cab design has stayed the same through the years, with a For Hire light on the roof, the map of London displayed in the cab interior, and a coin dispenser next to the driver. The dark leather interior was in perfect condition. I could smell the old leather and feel the history of this vehicle that once traveled the streets of London. She loved riding in her cab in local parades along with her poodle.

Mother enjoyed looking for a treasure, and she had an eye for quality. She once purchased a beautiful opaque dome-shaped glass ring from a dealer, and it turned out to have been made in France by Lalique. She was so happy to have gotten a great deal that she raised her arm in the air and then brought her hand down hard on the table, breaking her prize ring into tiny pieces. It was a big disappointment, and I felt sorry for her, but she said that it was punishment for her bragging. I knew Mother was a bit eccentric, but anyone knowing her would agree that was part of what made her so special.

Mother's funeral in 2004

My aura imaging photo

CHAPTER 7

During my job-hunting process in Minneapolis, I interviewed with Virgil Sorenson, the manager of passenger service at Western Airlines, and that resulted in a thirty-year career with the airline. Virgil and I have the same birthday, and maybe that had something to do with me being hired—we are both Capricorns. He was a man to be admired, very kind, and, I must say, very handsome. Years later Virgil transferred to San Francisco, and I thought we had lost a truly good manager.

My job was located at the Minneapolis-Saint Paul International Airport, and that led me and Katie, my dog, to live in a townhouse in Bloomington, five miles from the airport. One day Mother's husband came to visit me. We thought that was a good idea at the time—maybe we would begin to know each other better. I looked forward to the visit. First we had a bite to eat in a nearby restaurant. During the lunch, his hand dropped to my knee. He laughingly brushed it off after I expressed disapproval. That should have been my cue. After I invited him in my home, he grabbed me and began forcing himself on me. He won't get away with this, I thought. Feeling the pressure of his arms, I struggled to free myself. I was terrified and wondered what to do. Katie stood next to me, sensing something bad was happening. I quickly picked her up and held her close to me. He started yelling to put the dog down. I wouldn't, and he became very angry. Finally, he stormed out the door. I was shaken, not believing what had just happened, and feeling total disgust for the man. As bad as this was, I knew it would be equally hard for me to tell Mother what happened. When she was told, I'm sure she wanted to kill him. With the help of time, we were able to put the nightmare behind us, and we never brought it up again. Mother kept a lot of the trouble she had with her marriage to herself. It might have been pride or refusal to admit she had made a mistake. But no one would know what she was being put through; she'd be sure of that.

Western's reservation office was located on the level above the ticket counter. I worked there for twenty years—row after row of agents wearing headsets, very noisy, with every agent talking to someone on their phone. Through those twenty years, many close friendships were made, and twenty-five plus years later we still enjoy getting together.

Not until this point in my life had I experienced bullying. Thirty-plus women working in a close environment undoubtedly would at some point experience conflicts. I heard unkind remarks regarding myself and others in the office. I'm short, and I think I heard every short joke in the book. Later I learned a girl notorious for sarcastic remarks was taking medication for her depression, which would explain her lack of confidence and verbally lash out to others. I walked away thinking, it's the old "misery loves company" story.

In the mid-seventies, the movie *Airport* was being made right in our workplace, and it called for extras to help in certain scenes. Some of our agents had small parts. Our reservation office was used to film Helen Hayes calling the airline to find out if her husband was listed on the flight. The twenty or so agents answering the phones included me, and we needed to move our mouths as though talking but not make a sound. That wasn't easy to do, so I silently repeated over and over one word: bananas, bananas, bananas. Anyone who read lips would have thought we fed our passengers a lot of bananas. I received a check for $25 from Universal Studios for my big role.

Twenty years later, Western Airlines became Delta Air Lines. The reservation office closed, and I became an agent at the ticket counter, baggage service, and the Crown Room. I was happy with the transition, no longer sitting in a crowded room taking phone calls. My new Delta supervisor was fair in job assignments, and it was a fresh beginning for my final years at the airport. I was always able to live in the Twin Cities, which I was very grateful for, since many coworkers weren't able to stay. This was about the time when my friend Carol began her dream job as flight attendant with Northwest Airlines. She was in her early fifties, and was hired on the spot. I knew she'd be perfect for the job. She was based in Honolulu and assigned to the Asian flights. Years later, she returned to Minnesota and was based in Minneapolis/St Paul, where she was able to live at home.

Sandy Evanick and I were hired at the same time and went through training together in Los Angeles. Back at work we became traveling buddies. There was a $99 fare within Europe on SAS airlines for airline employees, and we made good use of it. One trip was flying to Paris and visiting major tourist attractions. In the Louvre, it was easy to spot the Mona Lisa. A crowd stood at a roped-off area looking at the surprisingly small painting. I tried to think what it was that stood out about this art; it seemed to be her wistful expression. Then off to Copenhagen, a stop we especially enjoyed— the many flower gardens, the lush green countryside with swans floating in lakes and ponds. Unfortunately, it was raining the entire time we were there, and the cold, damp weather would last for days. We agreed to not stay in Europe and got on a plane to sunny California to spend our remaining vacation days.

Before returning a second time to Paris, I joined a class at the YWCA in downtown Minneapolis and learned conversational French. Our group was all women, and our teacher was a woman who had once lived in France and was now sharing many of her experiences with us. During our last class, we ate at a French restaurant and spoke and ordered in French, which helped me to know how and what I would be eating in Paris. The restaurant had the atmosphere of dining in a country inn. The fresh flowers in small vases on blue-and-white checkered linens brought me to another time and place. We thoroughly enjoyed the evening together. After dinner we returned to the Y where our cars were parked. A fellow student asked me if I would like to stop at her apartment for refreshments; she lived nearby and I said, "Sure, why not?" It was a cramped older apartment building, and she was very sweet, offering me a glass of lemonade. As we sat drinking the lemonade and talking about the fun time at the restaurant, her roommate, or maybe I should say *partner,* came into the room, but didn't say a word to me. We were introduced to each other, but only silence ensued, and the woman never took her eyes off me. When I left the apartment, which was within minutes, I could hear the partner yelling as I walked down the hallway. She was obviously upset that I was there, and she made it clearly known I wasn't welcome.

While I was living in my townhouse, Western Airlines had a flight attendant base located at the airport. A supervisor mentioned a new flight attendant from Mexico City was looking for a place to live and wondered if I would be interested in having her live with me. Anna Hernandez was engaged to be married and wanted the experience of living outside of Mexico for a year before marrying. My little dog, Katie, was never so spoiled! Anna's half-English, half-Spanish conversations had me amused and entertained. I never knew what she'd put together in a sentence. She wasn't good at cleaning the house, mostly because in Mexico her family had servants who lived in a modest structure next to their house. However, I enjoyed the many Mexican dishes she made. She loved to cook, and chiles rellenos was her specialty. We enjoyed our meals together along with a glass of red wine, and Katie sat on her chair at the table with us. Anna was the person who arranged the design and manufacture of Western Airlines Fiesta china in the bold colors of blue, red, and white that was used on our Mexico flights.

Anna's mother worked at the U.S. Embassy in Mexico City, and she came to visit us. Anna and her mother looked forward to visiting the Cathedral of Saint Paul. Lyle Svedahl, a friend of Anna's and mine who also worked at the airport, offered to take Anna and her mother on a sightseeing adventure while I was working. He said it was interesting spending the day with the two Mexican women while they chatted away in Spanish. The year came to an end, and sadly for me, she flew back to Mexico City to be married. As she boarded the plane to Mexico City, I was so choked up. Living with her was an experience I'll never forget. Lyle and I both hated to see her leave.

Mother and I attended her wedding in the large Catholic cathedral in the heart of Mexico City. Anna was beautiful in her traditional Spanish gown. The cathedral was packed with people, and I noticed strangers were coming in off the street to get a glimpse of the bride. They sat at the very far end of the church and seemed grateful to be there. All along I was thinking how much she meant to me and happy for the opportunity of being roommates. We stayed in Mexico City a couple extra days for sightseeing, and with all the walking in the city, the heel came off one of my shoes. We found a tiny shoe shop built into the opening of a building along the sidewalk, with only a sliding metal screen as its opening. The man took a hammer and nail and whacked my shoe back together, good as new. We thanked him and continued our walk.

Mother and I always tried to squeeze as much as possible into our weekends of travel. Disneyland was one of those times; however, while there we were separated for several hours. I had just bent down to adjust the strap on my sandal, and when I looked up, Mother was out of sight. I thought she would be nearby and walked in every direction looking for her. I began to get frustrated and worried, and wondered, "What do I do next?" At the guest service building, I learned that she had already been there and had given the description of her missing daughter: twenty-six years old, a blonde, wearing a matching aqua outfit. She left a message for me stating she was returning to the parking lot and would wait for me at the car. Great! It was a long walk back, and by the time I reached the car we both were ready to give up the Disneyland idea.

The Marina del Rey hotel near the Los Angeles airport was a perfect spot for relaxing and imagining what it would be like owning the way-too-expensive boat tied to the dock. The Don the Beachcomber restaurant was located next to the marina, a true tropical experience. Our food was exceptional, and the fruity drinks with tiny paper umbrellas put me in the Hawaiian spirit. The restaurant building was round and surrounded by lava rock terracing down to a waterfall and koi fish pond. All in all, a great place to stay. In the evening we joined a nightclub tour of Beverly Hills, but our first stop ended up in the parking lot of the night club. We were told that too many people were in the building, and everyone from the bus had to sip their drink standing outside. It began to improve after that. At the Cocoanut Grove, our friendly guide joined the entertainment on the stage as if part of the act. Just being inside the building brought visions of movie stars who had once been here, most likely dancing on the large dance floor during the Hollywood glamor days.

Next stop was the Brown Derby. I was surprised at how small the restaurant was. The booths were tiny, and rows of film star pictures covered the walls. Our guide of the month had more drinks, and the others in the group were also having a good time, but I was getting tired and thinking it was time to head back to our hotel. Even though Mother's always a good sport, she too was beginning to think it was time to head back. Around two a.m. the driver finally decided to leave. As he wound the bus up and down the streets of Beverly Hills, taking wrong turns, I doubted he knew where he was. But I can honestly say I can't remember when I enjoyed a group of strangers more than that night.

Our vacation in Hawaii was much more uneventful. Mother choose the dinner, and our entertainment: the Don Ho show. All the grandmothers in the audience were invited on stage to sing along with Don Ho, and of course Mother didn't need to be persuaded; she was the first one on stage. She and the other grandmothers sang "Tiny Bubbles" with Mr. Ho, and her highlight was a big hug and a kiss on the cheek. I have to admit he was charming and knew how to entertain, and I enjoyed the show. For days Mother sang that song; she was a little swept up by him. In Hawaii she purchased a fragrance she would be wearing for years, Wicked Wahine, a tropical floral I also liked. I was always proud to be with Mother and proud to be her daughter.

Anna invited me to visit her and husband in Mexico City after they were settled into their new apartment. Staying with them was interesting for me; I learned the ways of a middle-class family in a different culture. Their main meal was midafternoon, followed by a rest time, then something lighter eaten in the evening. The portions were much smaller than the portions in

America. The evening meal, around eight p.m., usually consists of filet of fish with a fresh salad. Something I didn't expect happened when lying down on the bed at night: white powder floated from the mattress and pillow and filled the air with a strange smell. The next day I mentioned this to Anna and she said it was to prevent bugs from crawling on the bed. Somehow I knew that's what the powder was for; I just wanted to make sure and hear it from her.

It was clear to me that people with a lower income might work two to three jobs a day to make a living, and it also takes twice as long to complete a job as it does in the United States. The job environment and economic opportunities are much more limited in Mexico; on the other hand, building codes and permit requirements are less stringent. I was told that was the reason it takes people less time to build structures like highways and bridges.

Anna's husband gave me a tour of what they thought I'd enjoy seeing as I sat in the back seat of their car. I was shown the countryside, the steep hills, and the winding roads. Though we were being hurled from side to side in the tiny car, Anna seemed to think this was normal driving. I heard taxi drivers were even worse. I was hanging on to the side of the car seat and praying I would make it home in one piece. It didn't make any difference what was going on outside the window; I wasn't looking.

When the time came to return home, I was ready. While the plane was taxiing down the runway in Mexico

City, I couldn't help noticing a man, woman, children, and four dogs digging through stacks of garbage looking for food. While watching them, the image bothered me as I was sitting in the comfort of the plane, knowing that my food would soon be served to me while others were going hungry.

CHAPTER 8

Lyle and I were spending a lot of time with each other, we had been close friends for three years. He was always there to help out with anything Mother or I needed to have done. After having passed a three-year test of time, while on vacation in Alaska at Katmai National Park, we decided to get married. My cousin Pam and her husband Vern were with us. Vern was a Northwest Airlines pilot and very familiar with Alaska. He reserved our lodge at the park and made all the arrangements for our trip, including traveling on bush planes. Alaska was beautiful. It was a great memorable trip that included a close call with a large black bear that was walking toward us on a narrow path, but we made it to safety. Lyle was more worried knowing how dangerous it could have been.

On a balmy fall day in September 1972, we had a very small ceremony at Hennepin Avenue Methodist Church in Minneapolis. Pam and Vern were our witnesses. Our honeymoon was spent in Phoenix, but we both started missing Katie, the dog, so after only a couple of days we were back home settling into married life in my townhouse. It's fine being on vacation, but I'd rather be home in my own bed at night.

We received a letter from Anna saying she had left a wedding gift for us at the Miramar Hotel in California. Well, that was a little strange, I thought, but she said it would be held for me until I was able to arrive there. So Mother and I took off for Santa Barbara. First we landed in Los Angeles and rented a car, then drove north to Santa Barbara, but at the hotel we were told they didn't have the package. The desk clerk checked with the Miramar Hotel in Santa Monica, and that's where she had left our gift. Great! Back where we started from. The gift was a porcelain lamp—and it was broken. We picked up the remains and managed to have a big laugh over that long ordeal.

Shortly after our marriage, Lyle and I began house hunting, and we bought a small rambler on a lake in Prior Lake, Minnesota. We were thirty miles from work, and I hated the long commute. Many days went by, but I couldn't stop regretting the purchase. I missed my townhouse! Lyle told me, "We bought the house, we're not renting, and you need to get over it." Lyle can always make sense out of something I can't see. He grounds me, and I have to admit, sometimes I need grounding.

Our next pet was a little dog rescued from an Indian reservation in North Dakota by Lyle's sister, Gail. She looked like a miniature German shepherd with tiny legs, and she smelled like she'd fought with a skunk before arriving at our house. After giving her a bath and being fussed over with many bath products, she turned out to be the best little dog. She had little wisps of hair on her head going every which way, like tiny feathers. We named her Tootsie.

Tootsie no longer is with us. Now Lyle and I share our home with a black lab named Halo and two rescued cats, Coco and Sweets. A pet makes the difference between coming home to an empty house—and coming home. I know our cats are seeing things at night when the house is quiet; they look up toward the ceiling and seem to play with whatever is drawing their attention. I'm certain our pets' spirits return to be with us, and animals are very perceptive of the spirit world.

I found Sweets on the website PetFinder.com. I went through page after page of countless cats and kittens needing homes, but when I came to the very last one, I said, "She's the one!" I hopped in my car and drove forty-five miles to the Woodbury Humane Society. As though she was waiting for me, she reached her paw through the wire of the cage and touched my hand. As her paw spread out to me, I saw she had an extra toe on each foot—a polydactyl. She had tortoise markings, and her age was unknown, although I was told that she'd been discovered as a stray and had given birth to kittens at some point. She became my confidante and love. Coco came a couple of years later, all black with beautiful green eyes, also a stray. She suffers from separation anxiety and needs to be up close to someone. She's Lyle's cat.

Cats require minimal care; they're perfect for any busy or not-so-busy household. Unlike dogs, they don't yip for no reason, only purr, and they don't have to be groomed to be cute. My cats are kept indoors for their safety and my peace of mind. I can become mesmerized just by watching my cats do absolutely nothing. Leonardo Da Vinci said it well: "The smallest feline is a masterpiece."

Lyle left his job at the airport and began his thirty-five-plus-year career as a deputy sheriff in the Scott County Sheriff's Department in Shakopee, Minnesota. During his second week on duty he received a call on a domestic at a trailer park, and he responded alone. When he got out of the squad car, gunshots came from behind a trailer and barely missed him. The resident living there was angry that his two sons had been arrested for robbery and was out for revenge, wanting to shoot the first officer he saw. Minutes later backup officers arrived and the father joined his sons in jail.

Years later Lyle was the water patrol officer patrolling the lakes in our county during the summer and winter. I've made up my mind not to worry. I know he enjoys the job, and he's good at what he does.

Lyle tried running for a term as sheriff of our county, going against the current sheriff, his boss. We covered the many walking miles together during his campaign. All this while I was working full time, but it felt good being outside and meeting many interesting people going door to door and handing out flyers. There was so much to cover—the entire county! I kept going, thinking I would stop after the next block, but another mile would go by and I was still walking. At one house the woman stepped outside and began singing "Stand by Your Man" to me. She told me she admired me for helping my husband and gave me a lot of credit for what I was doing. I would have had her vote! At another house, the woman invited me inside to show me the dog they had adopted at a shelter. She said it was the best $150 they had ever spent. Yet another woman showed me the remodeling they had done. And I didn't know any of these women!

CHAPTER 9

I once read that it doesn't take much intelligence to get pregnant. I don't know about that, but I know it takes loads of intelligence after the baby is born, and no one but yourself can prepare for it. I was thirty-four when our first son was born, in 1978. Eric was a huge nine-pound, seven-ounce boy with bright orange hair. He was as large as a three-month-old, and started out on rice cereal. It was easy taking care of him, and he was always so happy.

I wasn't getting any sleep after our second son, Matt, was born, when I was thirty-six. Overwhelmed with work, I felt guilty I wasn't doing more for him. I felt I wasn't connecting with him like I had when Eric was born. My doctor told me that I was one of many women dealing with postpartum depression, a combination of feelings of complete worthlessness and depression. But I wasn't accepting that as the answer, and I knew I wouldn't become someone fitting that description.

One evening when Lyle was working, it was very quiet as I held Matt. I was thinking I needed help from somewhere. This wasn't who I wanted to be, and

I needed to get over these feelings as soon as possible. Almost immediately after asking for the help I needed, a response came from somewhere, and I felt as though I could handle what I was going through. Whatever it was, I felt it had put an end to the misery I was feeling, and I felt a relief inside. I still had a continuing sleep problem, but that was not caused by the problem I had with relating to my son.

Those years were hard on me. I felt I was at the mercy of babysitters who weren't thinking of the boys' best interests. Sitter Debbie only wanted friends for her little girl. That didn't work out, and neither did the licensed home, where the younger kids were kept downstairs and Eric was left to watch them while the sitter stayed upstairs. It broke my heart hearing that from the sitter's neighbor. I felt like I needed to suck it up at my own expense. It made me wonder: What was more important to me than taking care of my boys? Maybe this was something I learned from Mother so many years ago. My life was one big balancing act.

One day Lyle brought home a little red MG convertible he had bought from a county attorney. It was a big surprise to us, but it didn't take long for me to get used to driving it. Sadly, as fast as the excitement came, the disappointment followed. Lyle sold the MG to a friend of his who wanted to surprise his wife for her birthday.

I never knew what I'd find at home—usually an

old clunker that Lyle thought could be fixed up to make a few dollars. Lyle's side of the garage was never used to park his vehicle, only to work on one of these beaters, and I was always surprised if the job ever got done. However, nothing compared to the pink-painted bread truck he thought he'd convert into a camper. I regretted ever mentioning the idea of camping and fishing. I had thought the boys would enjoy it, but not in a converted pink bread truck. After that fiasco, we began looking at cabins for sale instead.

We bought our first cabin when the boys were young: set on twenty acres bordered by tall pine trees in a picture-perfect setting with a rippling stream. Time was spent wading, rock exploring, and bathing in the clear, cool water. The red outhouse wasn't too bad; it had an actual toilet seat, and I didn't really mind walking down a short path (except late at night). Reaching the cabin you had to drive ten miles down a dirt road through the woods. A quarter of a mile further was the clear lake where we fished and swam. We added a large bedroom onto the back of the cabin, but otherwise it was pretty rustic. The most memorable thing for me was my evening walk down to the lake. I loved the clean air, the undisturbed nature of everything, and the looking for wildflowers that I put into jars and placed on the kitchen table.

Mother spent a few days with us and had a great time. Eric drove the four-wheeler around the countryside with Mother riding on the back, her first such ride ever, her arms tightly wrapped around his middle, yelling, "Aaaaaaaahhhhhh!" up and down the hills and over the dirt road. I couldn't believe what I was seeing. She loved it. I showed her around my favorite town near the cabin—Park Rapids, Minnesota. We shopped, antiqued, and ate at the little candy and ice cream shop, enjoying its frilly decor. We always had a good time together wherever we were. Actually, she was my best friend.

Another image that has stuck with me is Mother and daughter having fun together in the stream next to the cabin. We carried long sticks and poked at the rocks at the bottom of the creek. We laughed as we stumbled over rocks and pebbles, splashing, our sticks poking through the clear water. We recited a nursery rhyme as we filled in our own words.

There was a crooked man who walked a crooked mile
Lived in a crooked house with his crooked smile
Walked a little dog down a crooked path.

Lyle target practices while up north. He sets tin cans along the tops of logs and target shoots. Each year he needs to qualify for gun handling to keep his law enforcement license up to date. While Mother was at our cabin, he showed her how to handle a handgun and had her aim and shoot at the tin cans. She picked it up in no time. I told her, "You look like Angie Dickinson in the *Police Woman* television series."

Lyle enjoys hunting, primarily for deer, and for that reason we bought some land, 160 acres for sale by a woman who had moved out of state. It's a pretty area with woods and a clearing near Itasca State Park, off a county road among tall pine trees, near to where the Mississippi River begins as a small creek, where people walk across on top of rocks from one side of the creek to the other. There was an abandoned schoolhouse on the property that had problems with people entering, even though No Trespassing signs were posted. From our house it's a four-hour drive, which prevented us from keeping an eye on the place. Afraid someone would fall through the rotting boards in the floor and get injured, we decided the best thing to do was burn it down.

Our first cabin by the creek was sold, and Lyle, Eric, and Matt began to build a new cabin on the hunting land, ten miles east of the park as the crow flies. The area seems to be very Native American in beliefs, and so far it's not commercialized. I'm happy to see it remain so and hope it doesn't change, although there is talk of extending mining into the area.

We installed a night motion camera in a clearing in our woods, and what went on was amazing. We saw the deer looking up and watching something floating directly above their heads: straight rods in colors of orange and red, and four perfectly shaped circles of the same orange color in a vertical line, seemingly at a standstill. We could only imagine what they might be.

There were also floating zigzag lines with what appeared to be feathers attached. The deer stood still and at times moved slightly as they watched the foreign objects, obviously not concerned or afraid. Some distance away was a straight rod half-hidden behind a tree that seemed to be aiming at a small white circle on the ground. We wondered why the objects seemed to be interested in the deer.

Other unexplained events happened at the cabin. One time when Lyle was alone, just as it was turning dark, he began walking toward the front of the cabin, and a ball of white light came out of the woods behind him. It bounced through the front yard and continued up a trail and into the woods. Then, poof—it disappeared.

Another time, one sunny afternoon, Matt and Lyle were in the open field that is now overgrown with weeds and grass. They came across two perfectly shaped circles, each approximately fifty feet in diameter. The grass was flattened, and in the center of each circle was a small pile of what looked like deer hair. Lyle returned with his camera and took pictures. That was one time when Matt was a little afraid to be at the cabin.

I'm beginning to think of the cabin as *Lyle's* vacation home, for the reason that something unfortunate usually happens to me while he's there. Call it Murphy's Law, or we're getting older, whatever, but either something breaks or accidents happen at our house when I'm alone. Once he called me at night and asked if I would check on something outside. It was a cold winter night with ice buildup on our front sidewalk, and not thinking, I rushed out the door. It happened so fast. Falling into midair, I instinctively broke my fall with my arms—and broke them. Back in the house, I picked up the phone and gave Lyle the information he wanted. I didn't say anything about my fall. I was OK until I was sitting alone inside the house. I began to wonder what would happen next. My arms were starting to hurt very badly; I couldn't even turn a light switch on. I sat and cried in the dark while the pain kept getting worse. I was unable to move either arm. Matt came home first and wiped away the tears that were running down my face, and then Eric showed up and drove me to emergency. In surgery, pins were placed in one arm and the cast was set in place, but nothing was done for the other. I was told one cast was all I would have, and the other arm would just have to heal on its own, with the help of a sling. Of course all along I was thinking none of this would have happened if Lyle had been home.

To my surprise (then again, it really wasn't), I needed to be back to work at the airport. No time off! My supervisor thought baggage service would be the best place for me to work, where I wouldn't be seen by the public. I was told, "If you need help with the bags, ask a ramp agent." However, they had their own work to do. My friend and fellow agent, Cathy (Birdie) Birdsall, couldn't believe I was back working. Trying to remove dozens of bags that are moving around the carousel with two broken arms wasn't easy. I also had the responsibility of retrieving the bags belonging to our passengers from other airlines with the use of a large baggage cart. But somehow, I got through those long months until I healed.

In 1989, the city water line was installed in our street, and our house happens to be the last house on the circle. When the line was connected and the main water line was turned on, a surge of water came shooting out in every direction, breaking the pipe leading into the kitchen, and our house on both levels was flooded. I was left to clean up the mess alone. Well, I tried. I got the job done as best I could and contacted our insurance company. I always think, there's nothing I can't handle.

Once when I wasn't feeling well, Lyle was at "his" cabin. I was pregnant and ached all over. That was one time when I was glad he was gone because I just want to be alone when I'm not feeling well. The pain was becoming worse, so I called a neighbor, who suggested she drive me to urgent care, where I had a miscarriage. This was an emotional time for me, and I faced it alone, but you know me. I'm the strong, independent person who can deal with anything. Later that night, I phoned Lyle to give him the news. I could tell by his voice that he felt bad, but that didn't erase the fact that he wasn't there with me.

What are the odds of something going wrong when he's gone? Pretty good. Lyle's sister, Val Roering, knows this and will ask me what's happened during one of Lyle's many trips up north. I like sharing my ordeals with Val; she completely understands what I'm talking about and agrees Lyle works too hard at the cabin. It's a perfect picture of a peaceful cabin in the wilderness, but too much work for a man in his early seventies.

I still call it "his" vacation home. There is a pole barn that stores the tractors, four-wheelers, Bobcat, lawn mowers, and who knows what else. He says it's necessary equipment to maintain 120 acres and to plant a field of grain for feeding wildlife and for a crop of some kind. And even before he can plant those seeds, the job of picking up rocks in the field needs to get done. But he says it's not work—he enjoys it!

There, I feel better now that I've said this. I was happy with our first cabin on the creek that was down a long godforsaken dirt road and ended up at a neat little clearing where Mother spent time with us. Now that I've said it, I can ask him, "When will you be going north again?" How soon my thoughts can change.

So, after forty-plus years of marriage, I'm glad we have our separate interests; otherwise I think we would get on each other's nerves (well, we do that anyway). He can be a challenge at times, but on the other hand, our differences make life interesting.

I realized our children don't belong to us when Eric announced he was joining the Marines. He has just graduated from college, and a hundred thoughts went through my mind. I thought he would work in the city, live near a lake in South Minneapolis, and I would visit him and enjoy the cute shops and coffeehouses in the area. That didn't happen, at least not right away.

He was stationed in Djibouti, a small country in Africa, at Camp Lemonnier, a US Naval Expeditionary Base next to the ocean. Eric and a Marine buddy spent time in the nearby villages and tried to help out where they could. Sometimes while walking along the roadside, they would be followed by friendly children. I began to send boxes of used children's clothes for them to hand out. After a while he said, "Stop sending any more boxes. The adults are also coming up to me and asking for clothes and other items I don't have."

After his deployment, Eric returned to Minneapolis and bought a charming Cape Cod with the standard red picket fence near Lake Nokomis, and I was let loose on decorating. He didn't even get upset after I painted his front door burgundy red. Our family pitched in and remodeled the house inside and out, ripping up worn carpet, refinishing hardwood floors, and putting up new siding. He settled into his new life with a good job, although he remained in the Marines. I loved frequenting the specialty shops scattered throughout South Minneapolis, especially my favorite Turtle Bread Company coffee and pastry shop on Chicago Avenue.

I was very happy when Eric and Susan were married in May 2014. The ceremony was performed while parents and witnesses stood together along the shore of Lake Superior. The weather was chilly, and a cold, damp breeze came off the lake. Climbing the wet boulders along the shoreline wasn't easy to do, and at times I needed help on the way to the spot they had chosen. Following the wedding was a celebration dinner overlooking the lake at the Bluefin Restaurant in Tofte, Minnesota.

After a while, Eric sold the Cape Cod, Susan sold her house, and together they bought a home four miles away from ours. I haven't missed my trips to the coffeehouses and boutique shops like I thought I would.

CHAPTER 10

My boys and I spent a weekend in San Francisco by
Fisherman's Wharf, a great place to visit and unwind.
We explored the attractions in the area and ate at
seafood restaurants. We enjoyed Ghirardelli Square and
the chocolate factory very much, but soon all I wanted
to do was sit on a park bench and take in the beautiful
surroundings. The day was perfect, sunny and still.
As I sat wondering what it would be like living in San
Francisco and staying there forever, a woman walked
up to me and sat down on my bench. We began talking.
She told me she had visited San Francisco years ago
and fallen in love with the city. After returning home
to the Midwest, where her family lived, she discovered
her life there didn't hold much meaning. She had once
believed that the epicenter of the world should be where
her family was, but when she realized that it was she
who was making the effort to see her family, along with
the idea that the highway went in just one direction, she
sold her house and moved to San Francisco. She told me
she was totally happy with the decision and has never
looked back. On some level I agreed with this woman

whom I had just met. Sometimes I have feelings much like the one she was sharing with me. I have to admit I was a little envious.

While I was the agent on duty in the hospitality room at the airport, I had the pleasure of meeting Maya Angelou while she was between flights. We talked for some time about how people's lives have changed through the years and being more afraid now than ever before. Something she said stood out for me: "The power of suggestion is very profound and can take someone to many places they didn't think possible." She dropped her long, dark fur coat over the arm of a chair and left the room, then returned with a hot dog with all the trimmings, saying, "It is as good as the ones in Chicago." When the time came for her to board the plane, she mentioned the television program she would appear on the next morning. I wouldn't see it; I would be at work.

Another day, I was checking in a young woman at the ticket counter. She appeared to be in her late teens and was overflowing with excitement. She was on her way to Chicago to become a dancer. Blonde, tall, she seemed a little nervous, and I was picking up on an uneasiness as she kept talking. Behind her I noticed two men watching her, talking to each other, and listening to what she was saying to me. Something told me that she was headed for trouble, and I wanted to help her, but there was no way I could, not even to say what I wanted to say: "Don't step foot on that plane." Instead I could only ask a greater source for her protection as she walked to her gate. It's amazing how we can connect to someone we don't even know. I still think about that young woman and wonder how she is today.

Once I was asked to help the agent in our downtown city ticket office in Minneapolis. The location was in a city center, filled mainly with stores and a food court. The parking lot was on the roof of the building, exposed to the elements, and it had stormed and rained all day. At the end of the day as I headed to my car I was thinking of the drive home in the pounding rain. At my car, I discovered there was a problem. A tire had been slashed. I went back into the building to look for the security office and found a young man very eager to help me. He handed me a huge umbrella, and we made it back to the top of the building. Out came the spare tire, and off came the damaged one. He switched them over in a matter of seconds. I wanted to offer a payment, but he wouldn't accept anything, only telling me to drive carefully because I was driving with a spare tire now. If not for him, I'd have been stranded on top of that building. I don't know what I would have done.

While I was working the Crown Room on a cold winter day, during the quiet time when there were few flights arriving, I was wondering about possible delays. The snow was getting heavier and I was catching up on entries in my computer. Just then our newest guest walked in, Rosemary Clooney. Her cheerfulness filled the room. She was pleased to have the room to herself and asked if I minded if she practiced on a new song. I told her, "I'd be happy if you did!" It was a Christmas song. She first sang in low notes, then in some a little higher. I enjoyed listening to her as I busied myself, trying not to be too obvious. Later she began talking to me and said how much she disliked being away from home, in spite of being obliged to travel. I agreed with her because I felt the same way—I too wanted only to be home at night. Someone once told me they thought I looked like Rosemary Clooney. I don't know why I mentioned this to her, but it surprised me when she said, "I'm flattered to hear you say that." What a sweet woman she was.

Another day in the Crown Room, I was clearing the room after the passengers had left and got a big surprise! My old friend, Gene, walked in. He had become a pilot for Delta Air Lines. Standing there in uniform, he looked amazingly good. As he said hello to me, I tried to return the greeting, and I got a little tongue-tied. I flashed back to the day that young college man had taken me on that ride in his small airplane when we were both eighteen. We talked about getting together and reminisce about how our lives had changed. Unfortunately we never did follow up.

As my sister, Matt, and I were planning a trip to southern California, I mentioned this to a coworker who had recently lost her daughter just before her wedding. I told my friend I would stop at the angel store in San Juan Capistrano on her behalf, and so we did. I loved the area of Dana Point, with its beautiful cliffs along the coast, the uncrowded tourist spots, and the vastness of the ocean. I have returned many times since. On that day while leaving the angel store, a shop across the street caught my eye, the Cat's Meow. I knew at that moment I would someday be an owner of my own cat store. I mentioned this to my sister, and she wasn't at all surprised, knowing how much I love cats. That thought stayed with me throughout my remaining days of employment.

When retirement became available, I was at the magic age, fifty-two, and I didn't need to think twice. I had worked thirty years at the airport and was more than ready to retire. I gave my uniforms to my friend Pat, and I chucked my Frankenstein shoes (Matt's name for them) straight into the trash. I could honestly say, "I no longer enjoy traveling by air, and the trips are a thing of the past." I had been to all the places I wanted to see and then some. I remember a pilot once told me, "God made people too short," meaning that we aren't able to see the beauty he sees when he's flying. I disagree. There is beauty all around us, and we are living in it. Some pilots had attitudes and thought of themselves as having a certain status. To ground personnel, some were called, "sky gods."

CHAPTER 11

When I retired, for a very short time I was an elementary school lunch mom. I was in charge of the condiments (mustard and ketchup) and was told to give one squirt on each tray. As the little ones came through the line, I began giving two squirts, and their faces would light up. I was told to stop giving the second squirt. I did what they said, but for me that ended the idea of helping in the school. The lunchroom staff was made up of rigid women who had probably been part of the school system since the school was built.

I began to research the ins and outs of owning my own business. I enjoyed every minute of my planning and looked forward to the actual ownership. My business plan was written, displays were purchased from shops going out of business, and I obtained a letter of recommendation from the president of my bank. I was fortunate to find two large old glass display cases trimmed in brass from Veigel's Kaiserhoff, a restaurant in New Ulm, Minn.

My chosen site was a small vacated coffee shop, plain and dark, with a coating of grime covering walls and floor. It was a bare space, a blank canvas, and we had our work cut out for us. I didn't mind that; I saw only the potential. I was very fortunate Lyle was so supportive through it all. He built a new storefront; the old one was a heavy metal roll-up screen. He placed new carpet over the worn-out tiled floor and painted the walls yellow and periwinkle blue. He did the construction work, and I made it look pretty, like a little cottage. I brought furniture from home; my antique Victorian settee was put to use for the stuffed cats and printed throws. I loved my feline shop, and best of all, I was surrounded by the things that made me happy.

One day I was approached by a representative from the Mall of America, who liked my concept and asked if I would consider occupying a space there. My answer was no, but thanks for the compliment. I no longer wanted to work in a busy environment with crowds of people, and the high rent was out of the question. I had exactly what I wanted in this small mall. A three-year lease had been signed at Cobblestone Court in Burnsville, Minnesota, an older small, enclosed strip mall with a weaving cobblestone brick path design winding down the center of the hallway. It had specialty shops and an Old Country Buffet at the end of the building near my shop, which helped bring in many of my customers.

For Christmas I decorated a Charlie Brown tree and placed a small sleigh below it. I advertised photo sessions for people's beloved cats and was surprised by the enthusiastic response. The little darlings were placed in the sleigh with felt antlers on their tiny heads while I took instant pictures with my Polaroid. This was a special time, when I brought my homemade cookies, hot cider, and coffee, always the coffee, for my customers. Each year I had a drawing for children for a large stuffed cat. I enjoyed seeing the winners come in to claim their prize; they always were so happy as they thanked me.

Searching for unique cat items to sell was always in the back of my mind. Minneapolis has a buyer's market, which I frequently combed for cat-related ideas. I came across a shirt that said, "I kiss my cat on the lips." It also was available in French. The shirts were big hits in my shop and brought out the snickers and smiles, many people admitting they did kiss their cat's fuzzy little mouth. Another shirt design showed a spoiled cat with the saying: "Don't wanna, don't havta, ain't gonna." It was bought by women who said they wanted to wear it as a nightshirt. They had their reasons for that, and I said, "I get the picture!"

I'm a person who's drawn to anything cat-related, and it was all for sale in my shop. I had clothing, jewelry, pictures, rugs, teapots, and much more. A bulletin board was available for people to post their pet's picture. It also had a few cartoons and the Rainbow Bridge verse for a deceased pet. My shop was one big cat house! (That's what Lyle called it).

Arriving at the store one morning, I was in for a

big surprise. It had been broken into during the night; the front door lock was damaged and needed to be replaced that day. I remembered Murray Anderson was a locksmith, among other talents, and he is the president of our Delta Air Lines Pioneers in Minnesota. He came to the rescue within a few hours and fixed the problem. Police wrote a report of my stolen merchandise, but mostly focused on the business connected by a door in my back room. That door led to a travel agency, the main reason for the break-in. They had ticket stock stolen, much more valuable than my merchandise.

I joined the National Cat Collector Club; meetings were held locally for the Minnesota Chapter members. We shared information about our collections and learned from each other, often selling and trading within our group. A shopping day for all local members was offered in my store and everyone was given discounts on their purchases—a happy day for everyone.

Occasionally a craft show was held in the mall. Sale tables were lined up all along the hallway and the public came in droves to see the crafts. I was happy that my shop also benefited from all the new traffic. I started thinking of new things to do with the shop, and came up with the idea of adding some old collectibles in a specific area. And that idea took off. A friend, Bev Simonson, offered to be my spotter. She worked as a reporter for the Prior Lake newspaper, and when out and about, enjoyed searching out and bringing me many cat items to sell.

Once antiques and collectibles were being sold in the store, I was asked to join a local Burnsville group, the Nostalgia Buffs. I learned a wealth of information from speakers around the Twin Cities at our monthly meetings. Some topics I never knew existed, like matchbook collecting, described by the fellow with his matchbook collection, and antique buttons (that was interesting). The woman told us that certain antique buttons can go for thousands of dollars. A man came to speak about his collection of old flashlights; he maintains a small flashlight museum in Minneapolis. I had no idea the topic of flashlights could be so involved. For eight years I've been part of the Buffs group; we travel to various locations trying out restaurants and have holiday dinners at homes of members.

We visited a historical house in St. Paul owned by a kind gentleman with a cat. Touring the main house with original 1870s furnishings was fascinating, but the basement was something beyond that. I had stepped into Slovenia. Beautiful hand-painted murals, costumes, antiques, and travel literature representing Slovenia—anything you can imagine. He had been a travel guide in his home country. I thanked him for his warm hospitality and said I would return.

While driving home from my shop one evening, I was worried about being able to pay the next month's rent. I couldn't let that happen; somehow I always paid the rent on time. Then something came over me and my body began to relax, and the words came through very clearly, "It's not important." As though the thought never entered my mind, I became relaxed, and the rent was soon paid. I didn't know it then, but this type of experience would repeat itself later on many occasions.

Multiple times the police were called due to what was going on behind the building in the parking lot. An adult bookstore was my near neighbor. Here I was selling cat toys while that stuff was going on a few feet away, and the building across the street was a child learning center. Halfway through my lease I was happy to see the bookstore closed, and I no longer worried about the customers they were drawing in to our small strip mall.

United Airlines retirees met monthly at Old Country Buffet. Nel, a veteran I knew from my airline days, often stopped by to see me when she drove a van for a women's group from Northfield, Minnesota. They made a day out of eating and shopping in the mall. She brought Maggie Lee into my feline shop, a true cat lover, and we became instant friends. Maggie was a newspaper reporter and editor for *Northfield News*. Northfield is a pretty college town. It is known for a certain historical event, the defeat of Jesse James in 1876, and has been voted the number one city to live and retire in Minnesota. Maggie had spent sixty-eight years with the newspaper, and was a community activist and voice of the historical society. Being the editor, Maggie included many articles about her beloved cats. She and her cat Princess lived on the third floor of an apartment building on Main Street. Though in her eighties, she was able to walk up the three flights of stairs carrying packages.

Each fall in September I set up shop in the large park up the hill during the Jesse James Festival selling my cat products. I enjoy this show, with the overgrown trees providing shade. Each year Maggie came to the festival looking for my booth. The last time I saw her we talked about the cute things our cats were doing, and her travels (which had become fewer, due to her health). I always noticed how well she dressed in her purple outfits. She liked to wear a large cat pin, often one she bought from me . . . and she always wore a huge smile. At that last visit, we hugged, and then she set out to find her favorite food at the festival, the crab cakes. Maggie died at the age of ninety-two. Many people would agree that her cats meant more to her than anything. She never married.

Years ago mother gave me a framed print, "The James-Younger Gang's Last Raid." It was the artist Bryan Moon's image of eight cats in cowboy hats. Each cat was named after a member of the gang, and the picture now hangs on my living room wall.

My shop had a steady business from the start, with little costs involved. My rent was $700 per month for 700 square feet; my inventory was secondary to that. When the end of my three-year lease approached, I was ready to begin working the outdoor shows, because those are where the people are. As I began preparing for the next phase of my business, my calendar began to fill with the show dates I would be working, and I mailed in the fees. Each weekend was an event of some kind: craft shows, antique shows, pet shows, and flea markets.

The large sign from outside the building was taken down and stored in our garage. Wondering what to do with it, we only had to look as far as the couple next door. They took in all the strays that came along. One night when they were gone, we placed the large sign in their driveway, plugged it in, and the bright lights of LOVE CATS glowed for blocks. It was their welcome-home surprise.

CHAPTER 12

The Minneapolis Gay Pride Festival proved to be a favorite of mine. People mill around in Loring Park, picking up the energy from all around. The park is filled with many colorful flower gardens, and paths wind around a pretty lake. People out walking their dogs stop for a few laps of water along the edge of the lake. Even though this event is against some people's nature and conventional ways or thoughts, it's one of the most peaceful locations I've been to for an event.

For three years my booth was next to the Minneapolis Gay Men's Choir, a great group of guys. That alone was entertainment for me. The men called me their Cat Mom, and that nickname has stuck. It was fun listening to their bursts of singing in harmony and just plain old having a good time. They took me out of my little suburban way of life thinking and opened me up to the world around me. All ages and families enjoy spending this day in the park. This would be at the top of my people-watching places. I recall the pretty young woman pushing her cat in a small pet stroller, getting everyone's attention to have a look at her adorable kitty, and the fellow wearing a long green feather boa wrapped around his neck as he wobbled along the sidewalk in his slingback heels. I wished I'd had my camera!

Complete strangers talk to me about their beloved pets, and I never get tired of hearing their stories. An example of the phrase, "Real men cuddle cats," was the burly motorcycle guy who showed me the tattoo on his arm of his Persian cat he so dearly loved. At the end of the event, a choir member laughingly said to me, "I suppose you will be going home now and saying to your husband, 'Honey, I have something to say to you. I will be leaving.'" However, when I told this to Lyle, he didn't think it was so funny. There are times I wish he would learn to bring out his feminine side! He's way too serious.

I may be going out on a limb when I say this, but I will anyway. When someone doesn't fit the mold she or he was born with, it may be confusing to them. That might explain when someone at an early age wonders why they feel mixed up in many ways. They may go on to question their own sexuality. I wonder if a reason for this could be that the person has had many past lives going on as a male and as a female, causing confusion in the present life. In any case, it's reassuring to know there is a presence that surrounds everyone and cares for them just the way they are.

I like St. Paul too. The biggest event in St. Paul is the Winter Carnival in January. People make beautiful ice sculptures throughout Rice Park in downtown; at night they are especially pretty with tiny clear lights twinkling inside. A snow queen and king are crowned. Next to Rice Park is Roy Wilkins Auditorium, where the Saintly City Cat Show is held. People bring all breeds of cats here from across the country, hoping to win a blue ribbon. Each year I am at the cat show selling my pet products, mostly handmade items: coats, toys, mats, and shirts that I make with my heat press. Along with my new items, I include a table filled with a variety of gently used pet items I have collected through the years. The money made from these sales is donated to the Feline Rescue shelter in St. Paul.

During one show a husband and wife asked if I would make a coat for their hairless cat, Buddy, who got cold in the winter. They wanted to bring him to my house for a fitting. Yes, they said "fitting"! Clearly, Buddy was their baby. I didn't want to discourage the sale and suggested they send measurements to me along with a picture of Buddy, and I would make the coat. When it was made, I mailed it to them, but Buddy didn't want anything to do with that idea, and he chewed it right off his body.

CHAPTER 13

Mother was active in her local Therapy Dogs International chapter and also founded the Good Neighbor obedience training school. She trained over 1,500 owners and their canine friends, some advancing to her service dog training. Her love was the French bulldog, and the first French bulldog obedience trial was held in Chicago in 1987 where Mother took over the ring in the exhibit hall, ad-libbing her entire speech on this special breed.

As she called the commands, hundreds of spectators watched and applauded after each exercise. Mother continued officiating over many shows through the years. In her mid-seventies, she started to question her ability to follow through with her commands. She had trouble remembering and said to me, "The dogs would be the last thing I would give up doing."

One day while I was shopping for fabric in Minneapolis, I noticed a woman carrying a tote bag with an eye-catching design of dogs and cats, and I told her that I liked it. She had purchased it at the Pet Expo in Mankato, and it turned out she knew Mother and was aware of the work she did with her dog school. She mentioned a friend who'd had her sheltie trained there, and I remembered both the woman and her dog. I've heard that if you stand on a street corner for very long, you will meet someone you know. I believe there's truth in that.

Mother bought herself a red electric scooter to use during her obedience classes to help her get around, now that her arthritis was getting much worse. Also at this time her journey with Alzheimer's disease began to get the best of her.. She had to stop training at shows and end her dog obedience school. I noticed she needed more care than what could be given to her while living at home, so my sister and I began to search for a caring place for her. Shortly before she left her home for good, she gave the scooter to her nephew, Chuck. He was the magician's son. Chuck was crippled and couldn't walk, only crawl, and lived in a building for the disabled in downtown St. Cloud. He said that the scooter was the nicest thing he had ever received. When we knew Chuck would die soon, I called him, wanting to know how he was doing. He said the scooter would go to his friend, who desperately deserved it. He told me, "Your mother would be happy knowing it gave another person his freedom."

After trying three locations, we finally found a memory loss home that was even nicer than what we had expected, and moved her there. Mother seemed happy, and I was impressed with the care she received; also it helped that a friend of hers, Irene, was living there. Irene had owned the Cat N' the Fiddle supper club on the outskirts of Mankato. They knew many of the same people in town. Irene was able to have her cat live with her.

Once when I visited Mother, I brought along my friend Carol, and amazingly Mother remembered her. We talked about the times when Carol was young and often came to our house, and during those conversations it was like time stood still. Often I brought her soups I'd made, and blended them for her to swallow more easily. As she ate, she smiled, and I knew she appreciated what I did. I looked forward each week to our visit, even though there were times when I needed to turn my face away from her so she wouldn't see me cry.

I spent many hours pushing her wheelchair along the walkway to the gazebo outside, where there were many beautiful flower beds. We would stop to look, and I'd name them for her and ask her if she had those flowers blooming in her garden. Sometimes I would pick one and place it in her lap. We often just walked in silence, enjoying the outdoors. This was a peaceful time for just the two of us. I told her about her great-grandson Sam, whom she had never met, and Hannah would be in our family years later.

In earlier years, Mother had said she wanted to will money to the local Humane Society in Mankato; she had been involved with their events and loved helping the animals. Her neighbor who lived across the street was on the board and often had rescued pets in her home; they had volunteered together for the shelter. In the end, I was happy to hear she had gifted a large amount, and her wish came true. The money made it possible to build a very nice new facility for the shelter.

I felt inspired by Mother's example. I believe many veterinarians overcharge for their services, even though they are aware that many people can't afford their high fees. It's not a win-win situation for anyone, including the pet, and so I came up with the idea of volunteering for the animal welfare organization, MN SNAP (Minnesota Spay Neuter Assistance Program) in the Twin Cities. We have two mobile units that travel throughout Minnesota providing a much-needed service at a much lower fee than what a veterinarian would charge. We mostly spay and neuter, which helps prevent so many unwanted litters. Also, feral cats are brought to us by dedicated people lucky enough to catch the stray. After the ferals are treated, they are returned to their natural surroundings to live out their lives. Often our unit travels to the Mankato Humane Society, where I also do volunteer work.

These are full days of strenuous work, beginning with the dogs, then on to the cats, and it's very rewarding when the owners return to pick up their beloved one. They can't thank us enough! Minnesota's Indian reservations are also served by the unit, and that's where the service is most overwhelmingly needed. We often spend a week there.

Volunteering in Mankato leads to some very

long days, followed by a sixty-minute drive home to the Twin Cities. On one of those trips, I became very sleepy and it seemed I wouldn't be able to make it all the way home like that. I thought of stopping at the next McDonald's for a mocha coffee. I tried singing to myself, opening windows, chewing gum, but nothing helped. I was getting sleepier by the minute and started looking for a place to pull off the highway for a short nap. But just then, I felt a quick, distinct nudge on the back of my neck, and I became wide awake. Continuing my drive home, I smiled to myself and said, "thank you" to whatever the source of that nudge was. I was becoming familiar with these unusual, special moments.

CHAPTER 14

When Alzheimer's started taking Mother's memory, she was unaware what was happening around her, in more ways than one. She had been an admired career woman, therapy dog trainer, antique dealer—a woman of many talents. But something very unexpected was taking place.

My sister and I began to piece it all together. It had started with Mother's second husband, who she married when she was in her late forties. He never really wanted to feel part of her family, even though he was always included in our lives. Now I began to really wonder why he had always seemed to resent her family. Could it have been Mother's two daughters?

During the time Mother was living at the home for memory loss, he was setting up a sealed tight trust. Everything the two of them owned, including all of Mother's possessions, were listed in this trust. My sister and I were kept out of her house except for one time the trustee walked us through. In her bedroom, I noticed her jewelry box had vanished, along with all her beautiful jewelry. I was devastated. I felt betrayed. Her jewelry should belong to her daughters. The front door lock had been changed, and I no longer could go into her house on my own.

We hired an attorney to help prove our case, which went on for a good couple of years of endless word against word. The trustee finally agreed that my sister and I could have a few items that had belonged only to Mother, things that could be traced back to when she purchased them. However, the antiques and furniture from her antique shop were locked away in a building to which we weren't allowed entrance. We don't know what became of those things.

Her sterling silver flatware was unaccounted for when a household inventory was taken by the trustees. When they asked me in an accusing tone where the items were, I remembered years ago Mother had given the collection to her grandson, Mike. She had stopped giving her big holiday dinners, and she knew Mike and Kathy would enjoy using the pieces. A doubtful retort came from the trustee, but I thought, great! If Mother were still living, she would be very happy the trustees hadn't gotten their hands on her silver.

Much later, after we agreed we wouldn't dispute the trust, all remaining household furnishings were placed in an estate sale in her house, one that was run by the trustees. The proceeds were put into her husband's trust. Mostly strangers and people interested in buying her antiques came to the sale, but many knew she had quality items and walked away with her treasures. My niece Lisa, Mother's granddaughter, went to the sale for a very short time and bought one of Mother's plates. It was a very sad day for the family. I would have loved to have received her holiday decorations, for the memories of all the Christmases we had together. She had that special touch in decorating, and it showed throughout all the holidays, even Halloween, when Mother wore a witch's costume with her black cape and tall pointed hat, smudging black cream on her face. Her dogs also wore little costumes as they greeted the kids at the door.

I made it known to the trustee that I wanted the containers of all her deceased dogs' ashes so that I could place them with Mother's. They were on the top shelf of the closet labeled with each dog's name. I was told I could have them, but as time went by, nobody gave them to me. I asked where they were and was told they had forgotten about it and didn't have them. What most likely happened is that they sold the valuable containers and just threw the ashes away. That was the one promise I had made to Mother near the end of her life—that I would be sure the dogs' ashes would be with her when she was gone. Her French bulldogs were her pride and joy, and there was nothing she wouldn't do for them. I'll be taking that regret to the grave because I couldn't keep my promise to her.

Through all this, there was the one happy note: Mother's longstanding wish to leave the Humane Society a large amount was carried out.

CHAPTER 15

After my father died, I began to get acquainted with my stepmother, Irene Barels. She started sending Christmas cards, year after year, including letters, which were thoroughly entertaining to read. She and her current husband, Bob, lived in Branson, Missouri, and each year they asked Lyle and me to visit them; they wanted to take us to their favorite shows. We drove to Branson one April, probably not the best time of the year to be there. Few shows were open, too early in the season, but we didn't mind. We like traveling in off-peak times—fewer people, and rates can be lower.

We checked in at a rustic lodge with a perfect view of a lake and surrounding area and phoned Irene to let her know we had made it. She was so happy to hear from us. The directions to their house were a little confusing, and the area around Branson has roàds going around the lakes every which way. But we finally found their house, a double mobile home, very nicely furnished, and we were given the grand tour and a story behind every collection they owned. They wanted to show us their favorite places in Branson and insisted on driving, though Irene was in her eighties and Bob in his nineties. There was a very steep driveway up to their house, and as we walked around the car, we asked, "Where's Bob?" It was like he had disappeared, and we had visions of him rolling down the hill. But he was fine. I don't think we ever stopped laughing.

The first stop was the Veterans Memorial Museum, where they both were very involved. As we walked through they gave us narrative descriptions of what we were seeing. Irene's complete WAVE uniform was on display along with her name and a brief history of her service. Very impressive was a large room displaying a bronze statue of servicemen that extended the entire length of the room. Later we were given a signed copy of the book *Return of the Enola Gay* by Paul Tibbets, the pilot and crew trainer of the B-29 that dropped the first atomic bomb on Hiroshima. We also received a photo of Irene and Bob; Captain Theodore J. "Dutch" Van Kirk, Navigator; Major Thomas W. Ferebee, Bombardier; and Paul Tibbets. Lyle and I were happy to spend time with Bob and Irene. They were so interesting, and I know our visit meant a lot to them.

Early in 2015 Irene's son, Ray, called to tell me she had passed away a day earlier. Ray had been going through his mother's address book for names to share the sad news. We had a friendly visit, and I thanked him for calling. I was glad we were able to talk, even though we did not know one another very well.

Our close friends living down the street were Dan and Gladys Ahmann. I was a lot like Gladys, and we were both completely the opposite of our husbands. Lyle and Dan are set in their ways and at times can be a real challenge. Dan said Gladys (he calls her Glad) and I deserve medals for putting up with our husbands for so long. I somewhat agree with that. After Gladys passed away, he sold their house, and Dan moved to independent living. They were the glue of our neighborhood, and their home was the meeting place where neighbors gathered on their front patio. Refreshments were always offered. Dan was owner and "Captain Dan" at the Chart House Restaurant in Lakeville, Minnesota, and the kindest man I have ever had the honor of knowing. I miss the dinners Gladys prepared while Dan played his old records on the phonograph, reminiscing back to another time.

Around the time of Gladys's passing was when Lyle and I got serious about moving. We had begun downsizing a few years earlier at a garage sale we shared with Dan and Gladys. Our house was listed, an offer was given, and we accepted it. Quickly, we began looking for another home. We made an offer on a townhouse and moved thirty days later. Everything went through like clockwork. I wondered if there wasn't a little help from above, other than working with a good female realtor. Now I'm adjusting to townhouse living and accepting the idea that less is more!

Lyle and I often go around and around over the

simplest of things; he can be so stubborn and will regard with dread most ideas I come up with. I remind him that just because he doesn't believe in something doesn't mean it doesn't exist. Once he questioned why I'd had a tarot card reading. I had just decided to try it that one time, even though I thought nothing would come of it. I gave a very short description to the reader; no names were given and I told her only that it involved a situation that was causing stress in our family. If nothing else, I wanted to hear what someone else had to say. I was told to stand my ground and make my feelings known and block out negative energy. I think of this advice when I'm about to lose control, and the tense situation soon becomes no longer a concern. Something I try to remember: if it doesn't feel right, it probably isn't.

One of my small pleasures in life is watching reruns of *Everybody Loves Raymond*, even if I've seen it half a dozen times before. But I keep watching, and Lyle asks, "Why do you keep watching that same show?" I tell him that it makes me laugh. Seems like there isn't a lot of laughter going on these days.

We love our road trips. We enjoy driving on the Wisconsin side of the St. Croix River and stopping in Stockholm at the pie and ice cream shop, where we sit outside on a bench eating the mile-high raisin pie topped with whipped cream. Another favorite of ours is the quaint town of Mantorville, Minnesota, where we explore the 1860s limestone jail and the museum in the old schoolhouse. We enjoy the Hubbell House restaurant, built in 1854 as a stagecoach stop. Guests have included Mickey Mantle, Roy Rogers and Trigger, Dwight D. Eisenhower, and Ulysses S. Grant. Not much has changed other than it has stopped offering rooms, and the sidewalks are no longer board planks. We have made this a fall destination when meeting my dear friends, Carol and Gordy and Connie and Ramon. Within walking distance of the restaurant is an opera house and antique shops and the chocolate shop where I buy the specialty, chocolate-covered potato chips. The entire downtown is on the National Register of Historic Places, an impressive status to claim.

On to Wabasha, Minnesota. I love this town, described as "the City of the Healing Waters" by Mark Twain. The historic Anderson House Hotel opened in 1856 and later became a bed and breakfast. It was also known for its cats! Guests could reserve their favorite cat for their bed-warmer. Seven were available, but the demand for the little felines usually outnumbered the supply. A woman who frequented my shop told me about this unique hotel, and Lyle and I drove to check it out. We found it to be very quaint and well preserved. After years of enjoyment, the hotel had to close; one reason was that a guest kidnapped one of the cats, and when the cat was rescued, the person admitted to wanting to keep their furry bed-warmer. The artist Bryan Moon has painted the cats of the Anderson House, a print I would love owning. Also in Wabasha, early in May, is the 100-mile garage sale, running in both directions along the Mississippi for all garage sale buffs (like myself). Wabasha is also known for Slippery's, the restaurant made famous by the *Grumpy Old Men* movies. Lyle and I enjoy the great burgers while looking out at the St. Croix River, and on the way out I buy a souvenir glass.

CHAPTER 16

Working craft and antique shows for many years, I'm becoming an old pro. It's interesting how the buyers differ from one show to another; at flea markets they will haggle over every last dollar, to the point where they're hoping I will give their favorite item away. And there have been times when I have. But the public doesn't realize the work we go through finding unusual, interesting items that will bring a small margin of profit to make it all worthwhile. Along with collecting what interests me, this has become a great source of entertainment and social connection. I meet other people who have similar interests. This reminds me of a word I like, *serendipity*, which means "bringing together valuable things not sought for."

The flea market in Medina, Minnesota is especially difficult. I set up at five a.m. while people are going through things with flashlights. It's all over at noon. Everything left over I pack and get ready for another show. I'm sure I got the bug from Mother and the eye to spot something of value that's resalable; she taught me well. Lyle's advice is: Keep things moving and don't get attached.

Now I realize my collections are diminishing in popularity and Eric and Matt aren't interested in anything I have. That's also the response I get from my friends in the antique club, and we wonder what we'll do with all our prized possessions. One advantage I have is the ability to take my things to the shows. But regardless of diminishing demand, selling at outdoor craft shows is what I enjoy the most. The booth space is limited, and I do the best I can maneuvering all my items into a somewhat attractive display. My Honda CRV is loaded down with a canopy, containers, cart, tarp, clamps, tables, weights, and more. But I love doing it! Each time is an adventure. Carrying only cat and dog designs makes it easier, and the only guesswork involved is shirt sizes and colors. At times I feel like I'm living the life of a gypsy, setting up and tearing down, each time at a different location, each one a new adventure and friendships. Living close to the Twin Cities has an advantage; most shows are within an hour's driving distance: Rutabaga Days, Lemonade Days, Raspberry Festival, River Days. A favorite is the Waconia Nickle Dickle Day held in the park near the lake in September, which can be a warm Indian summer day, or very cold—ten years of being next to the park bench, where my loyal visitors can find me under my blue easy-up canopy. There is also a large display of street rod cars lining the streets and the park, drawing another large crowd.

Sixteen years of selling at shows, and I'm still setting up my canopy and hearing stories people share about their beloved pets. Sometimes it begins, "I never knew until I found this tiny thing under the car or side of the road," often from men who never liked cats or dogs before, and their eyes well up with tears. Outdoor shows can be messy: snow cones, pronto pups, donut holes, and occasionally something unidentified that drips onto my table. Everyone's having a good time until a storm begins to form in the distance and I need to quickly put up the sides on my canopy and hope nothing gets ruined. I have been at shows where tornado sirens have sounded and we were advised to take shelter, away from metal structures. My canopy frame is metal, and that means I'm throwing things together as fast as I can and into my car to make an exit.

When it's over and I finally make it home, Lyle always asks if I made any money, and I'm always happy when I come home with more than I came with. That evening it's out to eat, my treat.

CHAPTER 17

Psychology held my interest in college, and I had so many questions, but kept most to myself. That was about to change when I was older and retired. I had begun wondering why unexplained events were happening to me, and whether other people were experiencing anything similar. I began checking into classes and found one taught by a noted psychologist in the Twin Cities: "Psychology of the Mind." It was a loosely organized, informal group freely discussing issues; there wasn't a fee, only a donation box. Its members had questions similar to mine. Our classes were fun, there were always treats to eat, and I was learning a whole lot more than I expected. Many of those buried questions were beginning to surface.

We discussed dreams and the possible meanings behind them. I shared with our group one that was very special to me in which Mother appeared, shortly after she died. It seemed so real, as if she wanted me to see her. In the dream, I was sorting through her pills that were covered with dirt; I looked up at her hospital bed, but she wasn't there. I thought, *Where is my Mother?*

and heard her voice say *I'm right here.* She was standing in front of me looking exactly as she had when I was young, and we were living together. She was wearing the grey sweater and red plaid skirt she often wore. Her brown hair was pulled back the way she liked it.

She looked so peaceful and beautiful. As we stood looking at each other. She put her arms out and we hugged. I said, "I love you," and she answered that she loved me. That was something we never were able to say to each other when she was alive. I saw her little white poodle, Sam, the dog she'd rescued from an old abandoned brewery building after I moved from home when I was twenty.

Many years ago, she wondered if pets went to heaven; she wanted to be sure they would be there. I reassured her that our loved ones would be in heaven, and they can be our pets. She was so easy to talk to on any subject. She could talk for hours, although there was one subject that made her uncomfortable: spirituality. Possibly this was related to something that happened when she was a young girl. She lost her mother at the age of three to a deadly disease, and her dad remarried a woman who neglected his children: Kay, Russ, and Mother. He was a minister, and the problem was never to be discussed outside the home. For that reason alone Mother moved away at the age of sixteen to live with another minister's family.

Some dreams are so clear, as if I'm aware of everything happening. I began writing notes and trying to make sense out of them and thinking there could be some hidden meaning. I was told to write everything down that I remembered. I tried doing that, but I didn't stay with it for long. It's not easy figuring out the meaning behind dreams; I only think of them as a reality check. But I won't forget one standout dream. It was so vivid, and I love thinking about it. It was very dark and late at night, and I was walking down an alley. Behind me on my left leaping over a tall stone ledge was a very large wolf. It ran a few feet in front of me and stopped to turn and look back at me. There was no fear, and I was very happy to see the wolf. It seemed normal that we were together. We continued our long walk side by side through the dark alley. All the houses we passed were painted a very bright yellow—everything was yellow, even the air. After what seemed to be a very long walk, my wolf began to fade into the distance and I felt alone, but happy.

During a class we discussed my dream and decided the wolf may have been the power animal given to me at the time I was born for my protection and guidance. This was to be a message I received while asleep. I learned we all have a power animal that was chosen for us. My wolf will stay with me throughout my life, and I'm to respect what I've been given. The meaning for a wolf is to be a teacher and friend. There are other power animals. A jaguar can be for power and transformation. An eagle is a powerful animal symbolizing vision. Horses are freedom and strength, and even a hummingbird can be a power animal for growth and evolution.

After my dream, I wanted to find more information on this subject and discovered Alberto Villoldo, who has written many books I find interesting. His books are very understandably written, and I've learned I have a connection with nature and all my surroundings. I learned to ask, "If I'm alive, then why isn't everything else?" And I discovered a unique shop in South Minneapolis that sells his books and other similar items relating to these subjects, Present Moment on Grand Avenue. A fun place to browse.

We discussed karma in class, an Eastern term meaning the Golden Rule, or what goes around comes around, the little life review projector that is built into our lives. In the end it reviews how we lived our lives in a fast forward motion, and we judge this for ourselves. It's as though our third eye is recording events we have to face, the good and the bad. Did I accomplish what I was meant to accomplish during this lifetime? I'm one who believes things will happen for a reason (almost everything, that is). It's what I do with these happenings and the choices I make that makes the difference. Choosing to be happy or just getting by will determine what an outcome will be. In the end, we will watch the little projector going through our story.

So how is this done? We aren't limited to one lifetime; we try to do a little better each time and stack up good and bad karma. The mind becomes conditioned by this repetitive cycle. I (my ego) is not the one coming back to another life; it's the soul repeating over and over into another life experience, repeating until I come close to getting it right.

I combined the psychology classes with another class being offered in South Minneapolis focusing on intuition. The classes could be called empowering, inspirational, and a little strange at times. We had the opportunity to have our picture taken by someone with an aura camera. The images were transmitted onto a photo, and the result was amazing. My photo showed color extending all around me, four feet in each direction in very bright pulsating colors. Each color has a particular meaning and subtly changes depending on the moods of the person. The outer edge was very bright yellow. From my neck down my body was red. Down both arms was bright green. We were given explanations for the many colors surrounding the energy field, and each student's colors were quite different. The color green is balance and calming; yellow is joy and freedom and nonattachment. Yellow is also a sign of highly active third eye. Red shows strong emotion and is physically based. I found this picture to be a quite accurate depiction of the way I feel and see things.

If anyone had told me these things were out there to learn, I wouldn't have believed them. Now I find there's an explanation for everything I'm experiencing, and also that there's no such thing as a coincidence. Lyle often asks what we discuss during a class. He refers to them as my "spook classes," and he doesn't know what to think of them. At times he can be very closed minded and likes to stay in his comfort zone. I tell him, "Just because you don't believe in something doesn't mean it doesn't exist."

During one class we looked at a past life. I was a bit skeptical, but slowly I began to relax and let myself be led wherever it was taking me. It didn't take long, and I became aware of another person. She was a young black woman. There was a presence of a man, also black, possibly someone she was employed by. I felt this was normal for the young girl; there was no hostility toward the girl or man. I was aware of flowers and a fresh scent of azaleas. I should note that this past life experience was occurring in the basement of a building where there was room for ten individual cots, nothing else. When it was time to bring myself back, I felt compassion for all living things, especially for that young girl, and in a way I wanted to stay longer. I think I must have endless stories to tell, not only from that life, but also from former lifetimes, if I wanted to explore it further.

Frequently I check out my favorite thrift shops and occasionally find something I can't live without. One time it was a set of eight crystal stemware glasses etched with a leaf pattern. They were pretty, but priced more than I wanted to pay, so I passed them up. Not long after, I dreamed of those glasses and how beautiful they were. Returning to the store the next day, I saw they were marked half off. I mentioned to the salesperson the dream I'd had, and that it was the reason I came back. She said, "There's also a set of wineglasses that match." I hadn't noticed those wineglasses earlier. Thinking "It can't get much better than this," I made my purchase.

Another time I picked up a certain feeling for no apparent reason. A newspaper article showing a picture of a three-generation family caught my attention. A Native American grandmother, mother, and daughter had been in a tragic accident, and the mother died. For some reason the article made me think of a family I knew, and I felt something was about to happen to them. Weeks later, my friend's daughter was involved in a car accident that took her life. I don't think there was anything unusual about this, but I do think messages come through when we least expect them to.

Yet another evening I was sitting on the living room floor sorting through a box of old unused greeting cards. I came across a card picturing a flower garden with a white cat. Naturally my cards are mostly cat-related, and that's what I send to everyone. I thought I'd send that card to my cousin Joann in Iowa whom I haven't seen in years. No sooner had I set the card down than the phone rang. It was Joann! She was thinking of me and thought it would be a good time to call. When I told her what happened, we thought what a coincidence it was that we came into each other's minds at the same time.

CHAPTER 18

My son Matt is now in his thirties and experiences unusual happenings. Together we discuss them and try to figure out what they mean. We don't claim to know the answers; we just like to see what ideas we come up with. At the opposite end of this spectrum is my son Eric, who is much like his dad and wouldn't admit to any such thoughts. Eric is the "still water runs deep" sort of guy, and Matt is the "fly by the seat of his pants" type. I'm very fortunate Eric checks up on his parents almost nightly to see how we're doing; we can always count on him.

I can be very sensitive and sentimental, which makes me vulnerable to pick up on things others may not notice. I don't bring it on to myself or walk around thinking about it; it just happens. Walking into a room I get a feeling immediately from others—it can be good or bad, but either way I'm soaking up their energy. I've learned to separate myself from this reaction.

During a class practice we were to relax and clear the mind and begin to imagine relatives who have passed on. The room was very still. My eyes were closed and I was thinking again, *Where is this going?* I didn't have to imagine for long; gradually I heard a rustling sound coming from the outer edge of the room beginning as a faint tinkling sound like chimes, then becoming deeper and louder as it moved. It lasted a couple of minutes. I opened my eyes to look around the edge of the room, but nothing was there. Others in the room were in their blissful state of relaxation and weren't aware of any noise. The sound gradually faded away as if dissolving into the back of the room. When we were brought back to reality, I asked others and our instructor if they noticed or heard anything strange, and they all said they hadn't. I almost wanted to say I hadn't noticed anything either.

I've finally learned how to fully relax, thanks to Amy at the River Valley YMCA, where I faithfully attend my SilverSneakers yoga class. All who benefit from her classes agree—we are so lucky to have her as our instructor. Amy added a monthly relaxation class, and I eagerly look forward to it. She places a drop of lavender cream on our hands, dims the light, and turns on two small heaters she brings from home. Soon we are ready to transcend to another place. Slowly Amy walks around the room telling a story with imagery, making it up as she goes along. She lightly touches my shoulder or arm with a gentle massage and to anyone else requesting the same. My heart rate lowers and nothing is important at that moment.

Nearing the end (no one wants to see it come), Amy brings us back to our surroundings. I'm so relaxed.

Friends Betty, Dorothy, Connie, Bev, and all the others, and I walk out to the parking lot and wonder, now where did I park that car? Too bad I can't keep that image I just experienced going forever, but the magic is gone the minute I walk into the house and reality hits me. Husband asks, "What do we have for lunch?" Oh, well, it's only thirty days until I return to that peaceful place and Amy can again cast her spell. My classmates and I have become close friends and formed a group for social events, including our lunch bunch that heads off for some monthly restaurant cuisine. We try to stay with family-owned businesses, not chains, and it's turning out to be a lot of Asian food, which we've come to like. There can be eight to twelve women carrying on about any topic whatsoever—never a lack of conversation and good times.

As long as I can remember I've had trouble falling asleep. I would lie awake one hour after another and my mind would play one scene after another. I can't understand how Lyle can be asleep minutes after going to bed. Then the snoring begins, which makes it even worse. I'm off to another room hoping that will help, but I still hear him loudly sawing wood. Amy has taught us deep breathing from the stomach and releasing the air slowly. Taking deep breaths is a big part of the yoga class. I never gave any thought to this before, I always took it for granted— the automatic slow breathing. The importance of deep breathing and relaxing my jaw muscle is my first step toward getting to sleep, unwinding my body from what the day has brought, and releasing the mind from tension and unimportant interruptions. I imagine my muscles relaxing, letting it all go, all the while taking deep breaths through the stomach.

I dismiss my ego, keeping it from entering my mind; I know it will return later. When this is done, I begin to focus on the background blackness of my mind, and often I begin to see color flowing through. Vivid purple or indigo blue and sometimes the two colors flowing together taking shapes of random spilled paint; it's beautiful to watch. This, I believe, is my third eye, also called the sixth sense, that I'm seeing. The first time I became aware of this I didn't know what it was. Now I look forward to it if I haven't fallen asleep by then.

CHAPTER 19

I was asked to join a survey in downtown Minneapolis. Everyone taking part was about the same age, senior citizens. We were asked to answer a range of questions regarding where we looked for help with medical questions. Everyone there was friendly, and we chatted about the questions we were about to answer, enjoying our catered dinner of roast beef sandwiches and fresh fruit dessert while looking out over the river below. Sitting at the long conference table, each was asked to describe where we went for health problems and where we got our help. Many answers were given: internet, local clinics, phone calls. When it came to me, I kept thinking that the obvious hadn't yet been given. Whose body are we talking about? My response was, "Listen to what your body is telling you. Monitor what you can on your own and look for changes that are taking place. No one knows you better than you know yourself. Then follow through with what it's telling you to do."

I left the building with a check for $60 after an evening of fine food and being with a group of interesting people. And to think I almost hadn't gone to the survey. I was happy I did. Not bad for two hours of my time on a free evening.

While volunteering with the mobile unit at the Humane Society in Mankato, I became friends with their local volunteers. One was Charlotte Gallagher, a nurse and acupuncturist who works out of her small downtown office practicing Traditional Chinese Medicine (TCM). I've had pain in my right leg for years and have grown used to limping. Charlotte noticed it while we were sterilizing surgical kits and offered to help me by applying acupuncture. At that point I was ready to try anything.

Charlotte specializes in animal care and has seen amazing results in those she has treated, such as the little rabbit that could barely walk that can now hop, and dogs with hip joint problems that can walk better. With me, I noticed a difference after two sessions and became a believer in Oriental Medicine. I was surprised there wasn't any sensation as she inserted a needle into my skin—she had a gentleness and confidence about her. As I lay there, alone and listening to the soothing background music, I realized there was something to this. I'm all for the knowing that I'm made up of energy and the inserted needles are moving the energy to the specific areas needing attention.

Over the last several years I had mentioned the pain to my doctor and was told it was due to a muscle spasm. I was put through months of physical therapy and exercises to do at home, but these procedures only made it worse. After years of getting nowhere, I insisted on an X-ray. The result showed osteoarthritis, the degeneration of cartilage in both hips. It's not fun getting old! I'm scheduled for hip surgery and will be so happy when my pain is gone (I hope) and I can go on my walks again. Behind our townhouse is a large pond with a fountain that sprays water high in the air. It's actually quite noisy and draws complaints from my husband, but I like the fountain and the serenity it provides. A winding path circles around the pond where I enjoy walking. My limping from the leg pain draws comments from passing walkers. I'm waddling like a duck, and they tell me to get my leg fixed.

I began researching for more acupuncture treatment and found a location nearby in Bloomington. The Northwestern Health Science University has advanced students who practice Traditional Chinese Medicine under the supervision of an instructor. At my first appointment, a very soft-spoken instructor came into the room. He spoke in broken Chinese, which made me feel relaxed. I listed the areas where I wanted to see results, mainly the arthritis and the pain in my hip extending down to the knee. A needle was placed in the side of the knee and into each hand. The hand treatment was to help heal my migraine headache, but I noticed right away that the knee felt much better.

At my second visit, the same instructor came

into the room and sat down. He looked into my eyes and asked me to stick out my tongue. I hesitated, saying that my tongue looked terrible—it had deep cracks. He smiled kindly and said that didn't matter. I was utterly amazed by how relaxed he made me feel. Not like a medical doctor bursting through the door, but quiet and speaking softly. Lying on the table, stuck with needles, I couldn't help but compare Western medicine to what I was experiencing. TCM has helped me in more ways than one. I have moderate scoliosis, which means my back is very rigid. Now I'm flexible and my posture has improved.

Years ago I saw a doctor for my sinus infection. That should be a common office visit, or so I thought. The doctor told me to remove my top. That should have warned me. Then he felt my throat and his hand kept moving down my chest until I said, "I think that's enough." He had a nickname, "The Captain," with yachting pictures on the wall. I should have reported him, but didn't. A couple of years later, I read in the *StarTribune* that he had been sued by a number of his patients. He's no longer living. How do these people get to the place they are? They must think they can do whatever they want, and no one will know. My heart goes out to all the young men and boys who were abused by the clergy. I can't imagine what these arrogant men are thinking—ruining a person's life, pretending to have virtue with a supreme being. They will also have to face their life unfolding in front of them, the good and the bad.

Mike, my nephew, gave me something to think about. The verse, "We must first love our neighbor as ourselves," could be interpreted as: "We must learn to love ourselves before we can expect anyone to love us." When we first accomplish loving ourselves, there is a possibility someone would see we're worth loving. There's some truth in that interpretation.

During an intuitive class and a time of relaxation, a fellow student and I were both sitting in chairs in the back row of the room when she noticed an angel standing behind me. She said the wings were folded down as if wrapped around me and protecting me. When the relaxation ended, she came over to where I was seated and told me what she had seen. This was a complete surprise to both of us. She was particularly taken in, as she explained that while growing up, she attended a Catholic school and wasn't very interested in what was being taught and didn't give much thought to it. She now looks at those years differently and has a greater appreciation for angels. I wasn't sure how to take this, but seeing her expression of amazement and surprise, I knew she was sincere, making me wonder how this could happen.

While driving home from class that day, I was thinking of the many stories written by people who see and hear their angels. I know my angel is there for me and wants to help; I just need to ask. I'm not put here on

Earth to be all alone.

I was told I would start noticing things I hadn't before, and that I would become more perceptive than before to the "outer world." That would become an understatement! My spirit guides decided to make an appearance from deep down in a dark tunnel. They looked up at me, then to each other, smiling. A white man and a black man. The black man wore a long-sleeved red shirt and dark suspenders and dark work pants. He seemed to be the one enjoying this more than the other one, from the way he looked back and forth smiling. His companion was more plain and serious. When they knew I was aware and seeing them, it ended. Describing guides in class, I learned most often there are two, and they are usually male. They had lives before and possibly we knew them at one time. The name "guide" is descriptive of how they keep an eye on how things are going and sit on the sidelines throughout life cheering us on or preventing something from happening.

During times like these and other times I think, Why me? Then I say, Why *not* me? Then I realize everything I need to get through life is right inside me, built in when I was born, with a lifetime guarantee. Knowing that, I should be able to get through most of the challenges in life I might face.

CHAPTER 20

In 2013, I worked a craft show at the Mdewakanton Sioux Community, a very large state-of-the-art casino and hotel. I was experiencing a very quiet day and began jotting down notes in my binder for this story. A young man appearing to be in his late twenties or thirties, the age doesn't matter, walked over to my table and sat down next to me and asked what I was doing. It caught me off guard, but I welcomed some company. He was tall, black haired, and oozing with confidence. He seemed very interested in what I was writing and began asking questions. I began reading out loud the beginning sentences of my story: "The universe has no meaning of time." "What happens in life is over in a split second."

I enrolled in classes at the Loft Literary Center in Minneapolis to learn to write, and what stood out was the importance of the first sentence. It needs to be a grabber. Just reading my first sentence that day, I realized that I hadn't done that. With the young man's help, I began to rewrite, focusing on the little five-year-old girl facing life pretty much on her own, and I began sharing more personal information about my life and my mother's than I ever have with anyone else. She used to say, "If you're not Catholic or Lutheran, you're going to hell in a handbasket." His comment was, "At least they have a handbasket." I told him that while we were living on a farm in Iowa for a short while, Mother was very unhappy. She hated living in the country. She would pray to be taken away with her two daughters by anyone driving down the road. Whatever I said to him, he answered with a positive response. I was very impressed by this young man.

His name was Antonio, Spanish for cactus. He had moved from Mexico to the United States and was currently looking for employment. I didn't know why I was saying these things to a stranger, but it seemed I had more in common with him than I had with most people I knew, much less had just met!

He was extremely knowledgeable in American history, and switching between his Spanish and English, I tried very hard to understand what he was saying—everything from the life of Albert Einstein to the world wars, even mentioning Rosie the Riveter. He stressed the importance of human touch and the lack of it. He talked about car accidents happening as the result of a need for human contact from people who were alone. I hadn't been aware of that. We spent most of the afternoon talking, and he offered suggestions for my book. I wondered why he was so enthusiastic about my writing, which I thought was horrible at the time.

His knowledge of the universe could have been the topic for the day, and while I was listening to all of this, I was thinking he would be an excellent teacher. What stood out was how positive and sensitive he was, and I felt inferior. I wondered who his family was and what had brought him to this country. Leaving the building at the end of the day, I approached Antonio and said, "You're leaving without saying goodbye?" He smiled, saying, "I won't leave until I do," and then he hugged me. I told him to have a good life, and he wanted me to have a good afterlife. He then said he would meet me in the desert someday and reached down and hugged me again. *What just happened?* I asked myself.

Later that evening I told my husband what had happened at the craft show. He said I was acting very different. For three days, I wasn't myself and cried at the drop of a pin. For some unknown reason, I had a feeling that at some point in my life (or a past life), I had tragically lost someone I was very fond of. While eating, which wasn't easy to do, I mentioned that the food tasted salty. Matt said, "It should be; you just dumped a load of salt on it." I found that hard to believe, because I don't use salt. Clearing my mind became the focus in the days ahead.

I was very relieved when these feelings ended. There are times when I relive that experience and wonder why I was so moved by someone I didn't know. What was it that came over me? Maybe one day I'll find out.

Each night around 11:15, my head is propped up against two pillows and I'm reading. Jean from our airline retiree group keeps me supplied with many books we both seem to enjoy. While reading my paperback, I hear the descending jets slowly fly over our townhouse as they approach the airport, right on schedule every night. I take a minute to wonder who those people are on board, and I ask, are they returning home or just beginning their experience? Knowing the hassle of grabbing bags and possessions, I picture the scene on board the plane at that moment. I am happy in the knowledge that I'm no longer a passenger.

Telling Lyle about a visitor I had one night, I wasn't sure how to say it. He has a way of making light of something for lack of an explanation. He replied that it must have been an alien, and said, "You're not writing about that, are you?" But I will write about it. It happened one night as I was about to crawl into bed. I had just turned off the light when something caught my eye. I stood up and faced a figure that I thought was the most incredible thing. I was mentally taking notes so I would not forget what she looked like. I say *she* because I was thinking this was an image of me. As we stood face to face, her smile is what stood out. It was serene and extended upward to her large round eyes. She was a pure white form with very thin layers of color circling the edges—red, green, blue. She was inches off the floor, and I thought I saw just a slight shimmering movement. We stood looking at each other smiling. For a while I did nothing, but then I reached out with my arm extending within a couple feet from her. She turned then, but kept smiling until she was gone. Actually, she floated away effortlessly.

Not knowing who I could talk to or who I would want to talk to, I decided to ask my pastor if he was aware of anyone else mentioning what I'd seen. He said no. But thought it was my inner being, or what I like to say is the essence of who I am.

I want to share a verse by Edgar A. Guest that I have saved since I was very young and have read so often. I know it by heart.

> *Life is a gift to be used every day,*
> *Not to be smothered and hidden away;*
> *It isn't a thing to be stored in a chest*
> *Where we gather our keepsakes and treasure our best;*
> *It isn't a joy to be sipped now and then,*
> *And promptly put back in a dark place again.*
> *Life is a gift that the humblest may boast of*
> *And one that the humblest may well make the most of.*
> *Get out and live it each hour of the day,*
> *Wear it and use it as much as you may;*
> *Don't keep it in niches and corners and grooves,*
> *You'll find that in service its beauty improves.*

To this Mother added the thought, "Give an idle person something to do and it won't get done."

ACKNOWLEDGMENTS

Lynn Cross, my editor. Without your guidance and enthusiasm, I wouldn't have been able to accomplish what I did. I can't thank you enough.

Stacy Lenarz, manager at the Savage, Minnesota Library. Always happy to help with my computer entries, which never were easy for me. A big thanks to you.

Jennifer Quinlan, Historical Editor. Opened my eyes to the very thought of writing and made me determined to keep plugging along.

Kate St. Vincent Vogl, author and instructor at The Loft. Having the patience to bring my memoir to life and showed it can be fun in the process.

Mill City Press, my publisher. Accepting my work and putting it into reality.

CPSIA information can be obtained at www.ICGtesting.com
Printed in the USA
BVOW05s1206030416

442789BV00001B/1/P